DATE & CHAMI

BY MARYAM MUBARAK

Dedication

I dedicate this book to the soul of my sweetheart and teacher, Mom … and my two dear daughters who spared no effort in assisting me, as well as all the friends in the United Kingdom (Scotland), New Zealand, Malaysia and South Korea, who tasted my food, expressed their high admiration for it and encouraged me to make this book, which contains some Emirati dishes in the manner my mother used to prepare them, as is particularly popular in the Emirate of Dubai.

Maryam Mubarak

Photography of dishes and old Dubai by: The Nostalgic Lady
Designer: Nadezda Skocajic
Copyrights © Date&Chami 2021
All rights reserved
https://dateandchami.com

DATE AND CHAMI

- 🟨 Introduction 06-09
- 🟫 Breakfast 10-31
- 🟥 Main dishes 32-79
- ⬜ Images from old and rural Dubai 80-87
- 🟧 Soups & Salads 88-101
- 🟩 Desserts 102-125
- 🟩 Beverages 126-143
- ⬛ Pantry staples 144-151
- ⬜ Story 152-153

Maryam Mubarak

dateandchami.com

Introduction

"A recipe has no soul. You, as the cook, must bring soul to the recipe."
Thomas Keller

I admire this quote, and it reminds me of the food my mother used to make for us.

From simple materials, she used to prepare recipes of delicious food, and through this book of mine, I will accompany you in a journey through my childhood memories of my mother's dishes.

I'd like to introduce myself. I come from the city of Dubai. It is a city of the United Arab Emirates.

Dubai has long been famous for trade in the Arab Gulf, the Arab world and globally.

In time, my city developed in a manner that encompassed all its aspects, which made it the focus of the world's attention, for its beautiful golden sands warm beaches, diverse markets, parks and restaurants that compete and excel in presenting the Arabian and international dishes to satisfy all tastes.

As for my passion for cooking, it stemmed from accompanying and watching my mother while she prepared food for us, since my childhood.

I remember that stage of my life well, when I was five. I used to wake up early to watch my mother milk her cow and goats and gather the eggs from the hencoop, and I used to help her gather them, and how happy I used to feel back then!

I used to sit next to my mother while she prepared breakfast for us. The courtyard of our house was spacious, and it had a big almond tree with dense leaves and a stretching shade. My mother used to lay the straw mat, put the charcoal in the brazier, and after the charcoal turned to ember, she used to put the baking pan on it to bake **Khameer** *bread for us. I used to watch her turn the pan towards the embers, causing the bread roll to inflate, and filling the courtyard of our house with its fragrance which is still stuck in my memory.*

She used to bake for me a small loaf she called a **Kowana**, *and I used to dip it in date molasses. My mother used to smile and remark:* **"This Kowana is to encourage you to eat breakfast, so that you can grow, be strong, milk the cow and bake bread like your mother. This is in the vacation, but otherwise studying is the most important."**

After she finished baking bread, she put ghee and date molasses on it and presented it to us as warm as her feelings!

We were a small family, consisting of my mother, my father and myself.

I learned from my mother how to make the ghee she used to make from the cow butter. I remember my mother's cow well, her name was Kashoona. She had soft hair and a bright white color, she produced a lot of milk for us, and my mother made from that yogurt, milk, **Chami***, ghee and* **Yeqet** *(hardened salty milk balls mostly eaten as a snack).*

My mother was a skilled cook, and so was my father!

I grew up between them watching them prepare delicious meals together, especially when we had guests. Whenever we had guests, my father would slaughter a sheep, and I used to be frightened by the scene of the sheep being slaughtered, so I hurried inside, hid and plugged my ears so that I could not hear its voice while it was slaughtered.

We had in one corner of our courtyard a large furnace, where my father would put firewood, light fire and bring a large pot containing the sheep he had slaughtered to cook it. Then, my mother and father would begin preparing the feast for the guests, and once the meal was prepared, my mother would also share some of it with our neighbors and friends, as is the custom of the people of my country in particular and the Arab Gulf in general.

After I became nine years old, my mother began teaching me some simple meals, like eggs and tomatoes for breakfast. I did not face any difficulty in learning, which is due to my passion to learn cooking from watching my mother prepare the food. I used to record everything I watched in my mind, and then in my little notebook, and when my mother left the house, I used to go to the kitchen and prepare some of the meals she taught me. When she came back, she was very delighted when she tasted my food. She used to worry about me handling the knife and lighting the stove, but because of my cautious behavior, she used to allow me to prepare some simple and easy meals.

My father used to work as a diver searching for pearls, and that occupation made him be away for months. However, after my birth, he settled for working in commerce and travelling across some Gulf countries, which helped him become acquainted with some ways of cooking some meals that were not popular in my country, and he later prepared some of them for us, such as **Momawash** *and* **Murabyan***. These two meals are famous in Kuwait and Bahrain, and my mother became very good at making them, as well as* **Uqaili ring (cake)** *and* **Uruq disk (bread)***.*

I will include some of these delicious meals in my book, alongside the meals my mother used to prepare for us with their old ingredients that were available in the 1970s, which are still prepared in every Emirati house and some across the Arab Gulf.

These meals underwent some developments and updates in terms of the method of preparation and presentation. Nevertheless, I will present them to you as my mother used to make them, preserving the heritage of my country and including some of my mother's stories. It is my pleasure to present them to you through this book of mine, so that you can get to know them and the recipe to make them, try them yourself and taste the old Emirati food without any modifications.

I was keen on presenting them to you in an easy and simplified manner, considering the availability of all their ingredients in global stores, whether large or small.

Some of our food traditions and customs

Among our customs and traditions that are inherited to this day is sending some of the home-prepared food to the neighbors or friends, which increases love and affability. The food container presented to neighbors or friends must not be returned empty, for this is considered inappropriate or stingy behavior and it annoys people. The one presented with food must, in the nearest opportunity, put something in the container, even something simple like dates for example.

The container in which food is sent must be clean and free from scratches or cracks, and for the affluent families, a new container is used and it represents their financial or social status. We have a passed-down pronoun saying: "Whoever eats alone, chokes." It means that we must share the food with our loved ones, as well as the poor. Exchanging food increases on happy occasions, in the blessed month of Ramadan, Eid Al-Fitr and Eid Al-Adha.

Our traditions also include sending a multi-course meal to those returning from medical treatment or travel. As for the people returning from pilgrimage, they are honored by sending food to them alongside live cattle, as a warm reception to them for returning safely from the rituals of pilgrimage.

In summer, exchanging fresh ripe dates and some of the available fruits, such as melons, mangos and lemons, among friends is also a followed tradition here.

I am delighted to escort you on a journey through the pages of this book of mine, to introduce you to some of the dishes my mother used to prepare for us, including some memories that are still stuck in my mind.

Ryoog (Breakfast)

Chami

BREAKFAST  Vegetarian

» Chami is a dairy product, and it somewhat resembles cottage cheese. It is considered a traditional meal. In Dubai it is eaten with dates, and it is popular among the young and the old alike. The following recipe explains the preparation of Chami in a simplified manner, so that you can prepare at your home and enjoy it, preferably with dates.

Personally, I tend to eat it by sprinkling some ghee on it and putting it in the middle of the date fruit, so that the Chami's salty taste gets mixed with the sweetness of the dates, and the richness of the ghee flavor.

 **INGREDIENTS**

- 2 × 500g yogurt boxes (1000g in total)
- 500ml of water
- ½ teaspoon of salt

 **DIRECTIONS**

1. Mix the yogurt and the water with a hand whisk until they become intermixed but without froth.
2. Add the salt to the mixture and mix it in gently.
3. Pour the mix in a non-stick pot that is clean and free of food smells.
4. Put it on medium heat without any stirring for 40 minutes.
5. After that, a disk separated from the water should form (float) on its surface. Once that happens, turn off the stove and leave the Chami to cool down completely, drain it gently in a fine sieve and leave it until it gets rid of the water completely.
6. Place the Chami in a clean container with a tight lid and preserve it in the fridge.
7. It is traditionally presented after sprinkling it with ghee, and it is eaten with dates.

 **Note:** Chami is usually made from Laban (salty liquid yoghurt) that is available in all markets in Arab Gulf countries, but I chose to make it from yogurt, because laban may not be available in many markets around the world.

LEVEL OF DIFFICULTY

Balaleet 1

BREAKFAST  Vegetarian

» Balaleet is considered among the traditional meals in most countries of the Arab Gulf. It is served on special occasions and also for breakfast. The vermicelli used in preparing it is available in Asian shops in most countries. This is my mother's recipe for the Balaleet meal.

INGREDIENTS

10+20 minutes PREP TIME + COOKING

- 200g of vermicelli
- A small onion, finely-chopped
- A 1/2 cup of sugar
- 3 eggs, whisked with half a teaspoon of salt
- 4 tablespoons of ghee
- 5 cups off water
- 1 teaspoon of fine cardamom powder
- ¼ teaspoon of cinnamon
- ¼ teaspoon of turmeric
- ¼ teaspoon of saffron, soaked in a ¼ cup of rose water*
- 2 tablespoons of vegetable oil

 DIRECTIONS

1. Pour 2 liters of water in a pot on the stove and add 2 tablespoons of oil (to prevent the vermicelli from sticking and lumping up).

2. When the water reaches the boiling point, put the vermicelli in and stir it. After 3 minutes, drain the water off of it in a sieve, then add ¾ of the sugar to it while it is still in the sieve, mix the sugar gently with the vermicelli and then cover it.

3. In the same pot (from step 1 and 2) and after the water dries up, put the ghee, then add the onion, stir it and change the heat to low until the onion becomes golden-colored.

4. Add the cardamom, the turmeric and the cinnamon to the onion and stir.

5. Add the eggs right afterwards and stir until the egg breaks into fragments, after that put back the cooked and drained vermicelli (i.e. from step 2) and mix them all together.

6. Add the remaining sugar and sprinkle the mixture with the rose-water-soaked saffron. Then cover the pot tightly and leave it on low heat for 6 minutes.

7. Mix the Balaleet one more time, and then it is ready to serve.

LEVEL OF DIFFICULTY

 **Note**: The cooking duration in step 1 is not fixed, as if the Vermicilli is thick, additional 5-6 minutes might be needed. As for the sugar, it can be reduced if desired.

*Make sure to double check that it is rose water that you are using and not the more widely used orange blossom water.

DATE AND CHAMI - BREAKFAST

Balaleet Magli
(Fried Balaleet) 2

 BREAKFAST Vegetarian

 This is another way to make the Balaleet meal.

 10+25 minutes PREP TIME + COOKING

INGREDIENTS

- 1 ½ cup of vermicelli
- ½ cup of sugar
- ½ tablespoon of fine cardamom powder
- 6 cups of hot water
- ½ cup of vegetable oil
- ½ teaspoon of saffron, soaked in 5 tablespoons of rose water
- 3 tablespoons of ghee
- 3 eggs, whisked with ¼ teaspoon of salt or as desired
- 2 to 3 tablespoons of ghee to fry the eggs

DIRECTIONS

1. Fry the vermicelli in a ½ cup of oil until it becomes golden-colored, then add the hot water and leave it on medium heat for 5-7 minutes.

2. Drain the water off of the vermicelli using a sieve, and then return the vermicelli back in the pot, add the sugar and the cardamom, mix them all together, flatten the surface of the mixture, then sprinkle the rose water and the saffron and the 3 tablespoons of ghee, cover the pot and leave it on low heat for 8 minutes.

3. Fry the whisked egg in two tablespoons of ghee, put the Balaleet in the serving plate and then place the fried egg on top of it.

 **Note:** The fried Balaleet may need longer cooking time (step 1) than the normal Balaleet, because after frying it, its texture becomes more solid.

 LEVEL OF DIFFICULTY

Baidh wa tomat

BREAKFAST
Vegetarian

(Eggs and Tomatoes)

> When I was little, we had a barn in our house where my mother raised cows, sheep and hens. On somedays, I used to help her gather the eggs in the morning, that she would then use in cooking Baidh wa tomat for our breakfast. It is a delicious breakfast meal that is widely common in my home country, it is usually served with Arabic bread or any type of bread, it could also be used as a sandwich filling.

INGREDIENTS

- 5 eggs, whisked
- 1 onion, cut into small cubes
- 4 tomatoes, cut into small cubes
- 5 tablespoons of ghee or butter
- 1 teaspoon of cumin powder
- 1 teaspoon of Kabsa spices (if available)
- ¼ teaspoon of red chili (or as desired)
- 1 teaspoon of salt (or as desired)

DIRECTIONS

1. Fry the onion in the ghee.
2. After it withers and gains a golden shade, add the tomatoes to it and leave them on medium heat until the tomatoes dissolve completely (around 3 minutes).
3. After that season it with cumin, Kabsa spices, red chili and finally salt, then stir the mix on low heat for two minutes.
4. Then, add the eggs while stirring continuously until they are cooked. The final cooking takes around 3 minutes.
5. It is served with Arabic bread or any other type of bread preferred by you.

DATE AND CHAMI - BREAKFAST

Chebab Bread

BREAKFAST  Vegetarian

> It resembles pancakes in shape, but it tastes differently. It is one of the delicious traditional bakeries. It is spread with ghee and served with date molasses or honey, it could also be sprinkled with sugar. It is usually served for breakfast.

INGREDIENTS

90+60 minutes PREP TIME + COOKING

- 1 ½ cups of Chakki Atta flour (or Nan Bread flour)
- 2 eggs
- 2 tablespoons of sugar
- 2 tablespoons of vegetable oil
- 1 ½ tablespoon of instant yeast
- ½ tablespoon of cardamom powder
- ¼ teaspoon of saffron
- ¼ tablespoon of salt
- 1 1/4 cup of water for kneading
- Date molasses to serve

DIRECTIONS

1. Put the flour in a bowl, add to it all the dry ingredients and the sugar, and mix them well.
2. Add the liquid ingredients, mix them all either by hand or by an electric mixer until a soft dough forms. Leave the dough sit for 2 hours to rest well.
3. Put a non-stick frying pan on medium heat and spray it with a bit of oil.
4. Take about ¼ to ⅓ a cup of the dough (depending on the pan size), pour it in the pan and shake it a little until it fills the bottom of the pan.
5. Leave it until the disk becomes filled with holes and solidifies, then sprinkle half a teaspoon of ghee on it, flip it on the other side, then take it out of the pan when both sides are somewhat reddish.
6. Repeat until the dough is used up.

LEVEL OF DIFFICULTY

 *Note* — The dough (step 2) should lie somewhere between liquid and squishy.

DATE AND CHAMI - BREAKFAST

Khameer Bread

BREAKFAST — Vegetarian

> *This bread is considered to be what distinguishes my country from the rest of the Arab Gulf countries. It is popular among the young before the old. My mother was skilled in making it, and watching her baking it is one of my fondest childhood memories. What a wonderful smell it had when baked in the ancient traditional way on charcoal or in the furnace! It is considered a breakfast dish, and it is usually spread with ghee, and served with date molasses, honey and cheese.*
>
> *Anciently, the baking pan is placed on embers while the baker prepares the dough for baking, which is done by spreading the dough into multiple disks and dampening the bottom side of the disks with water. Each disk is then placed on the baking pan and the pan is flipped upside down so that the desk faces the ember (the dampening water helps the desk stay in place when the pan is flipped). After that, the face of the dough was spread with eggs, sprinkled with sesame, flipped again to face the embers, and left for some minutes until it was inflated and turned golden-colored. Then it was spread with ghee and served. Over the years, the method for baking Khameer bread evolved, and it is now baked in a special electric pot. The face is spread with eggs and sprinkled with sesame, black seed or thyme, and then the pot is closed. As for whoever does not have the special pot, it can be baked in an oven or bread maker. Also, in the following recipe, I have tried to simplify the baking method due to the unavailability of the container in which it is baked at international markets. This bread has a wide popularity in my country that can be likened to, for example, the popularity of scones in the United Kingdom.*

INGREDIENTS

- 1 cup of white flour
- 1 cup of Chakki Atta flour (or Nan bread flour)
- 3 tablespoons of vegetable oil
- 150 gm of pitted dates soaked in one cup of warm water
- ½ tablespoon of fennel (seeds)
- A sprinkle or ½ teaspoon of salt
- 2 tablespoons of instant yeast
- ¼ cup of warm water
- ¼ tablespoon of sugar
- 1 egg, whisked with 1 teaspoon of rose water
- Ghee to spread on the bread after getting it out of the oven

DIRECTIONS

1. Put the yeast in the warm water and add ¼ a tablespoon of sugar to it, and leave it until the yeast rises. Meanwhile, mix the dates with the water it is soaked-in well and then strain it through a sieve so that a smooth puree is obtained.

2. Mix the flour well with the Chakki Atta flour, the fennel, the oil, the salt, the risen yeast, and the date puree. Mix everything together well and start kneading until a soft and cohesive dough forms (you might need to add about 1/4 cup or less of water to reach this state). Leave the dough set for 90 minutes in a warm place.

3. Form the dough into 10 balls and start spreading them into disks with a diameter of about 13cm each.

4. Place the disks in an oven tray, spread the disks surfaces with whisked eggs, sprinkle them with sesame or black seed, put the tray in the oven and bake for 10 minutes on a 180° Celsius temperature.

5. The bread is then sprinkled with ghee, and eaten with date molasses and cream cheese.

DATE AND CHAMI - BREAKFAST

Dango or Nakhi (Chickpeas)

 **BREAKFAST** — Vegan

>> It is a type of beans and we eat it a lot in my country and the Arab Gulf countries, especially for breakfast and dinner.

 180+60 minutes PREP TIME + COOKING

INGREDIENTS

- 2 cups of chickpeas, soaked in 2 liters of water and 1 teaspoon of baking powder for three hours (traditionally, it is soaked for a full night and cooked in the early morning. But nowadays, its preparation has become easier and faster, due to the availability of pressure cookers. Also adding baking powder when soaking it speeds up its cooking.)
- 2 teaspoons of cumin seeds
- 10 dried small round red chili wholes (shown in page 144)
- 1 ½ Tablespoon of salt or as desired

DIRECTIONS

1. After the soaking, put 2 liters of water in a pot on the stove, and when the water boils, add the chickpeas.
2. After 30 more minutes, add the cumin, the red chili and the salt.
3. After another 20-30 minutes, it is now cooked. Scoop it in a serving bowl, squeeze lemon on top of it and serve it.

 LEVEL OF DIFFICULTY

Khobz Magly

BREAKFAST
Vegetarian

(Fried Bread)

> My mother used to prepare this type of bread for us in the early 1980s, therefore, it is generally considered of the newer types of bread, we used to eat it particularly in the winter, as eaten hot, it brings in a nice and warm felling of comfort.

90+45 minutes
PREP TIME + COOKING

INGREDIENTS

- 2 cups of white flour
- 1 ½ tablespoon of instant yeast
- 4 tablespoons of powdered milk
- ½ tablespoon of salt
- 2 eggs, whisked
- 2 tablespoons of vegetable oil
- 1 teaspoon of fennel seeds
- 1 teaspoon of cardamom powder
- ½ teaspoon of saffron
- ¼ cup of warm water
- ½ cup of sugar
- Water for kneading
- Oil for deep frying

DIRECTIONS

1. Put the yeast and a little bit of sugar in the warm water, and leave it aside.
2. Put the flour in the a bowl and add all the dry ingredients to it.
3. Mix them together, then add the oil and mix it with the rest of the ingredients.
4. Add the eggs and the yeast and sugar mix and begin kneading. As for the water, add it little by little until the dough becomes cohesive and not squishy.
5. Shape the dough into a ball, spread a bit of oil on its surface, then put it in a warm place for 90-120 minutes to rest.
6. After the dough rests, shape it into balls each the size of a lemon, then spread each ball into an average-sized disk.
7. After that, pour the oil in a large frying pan (suitable for deep frying). After the oil heats up, fry the bread disks in it until they become inflated and golden-colored.
8. The bread is then served with creamy cheese or honey.

LEVEL OF DIFFICULTY

DATE AND CHAMI - BREAKFAST

Bajela
(Fava Beans)

BREAKFAST — **Vegan**

>> This simple dish is famous in most Arab Gulf countries and it is mostly eaten for breakfast.

Overnight PREP TIME

45+50 minutes COOKING

INGREDIENTS

- 2 cups of broad fava beans
- 2 liters of water
- 2 teaspoons of salt (or as desired)

DIRECTIONS

1. Soak the beans for a full night in warm water.
2. The next morning, pour 2 liters of water in a pot and add the soaked beans to it, leave it cooking on medium heat.
3. After 30 minutes, when it is half cooked, add the salt and leave it on low heat for another 30 minutes.

Note: The overall cooking time may take an hour or bit longer depending on the hardness of the beans, therefore, a pressure cooker could be used to save time and effort.

LEVEL OF DIFFICULTY

Baidh bil basal
(Eggs with Onion)

BREAKFAST — Vegetarian

» *My mother used to prepare this type of eggs for us with simple ingredients. However, it had a wonderful taste.*

10+15 minutes PREP TIME + COOKING

INGREDIENTS

- 5 eggs
- 1 average-sized onion, chopped to medium sized cubes
- 1 Red chili, finely chopped (optional)
- 2 cloves of garlic, crushed
- 1 teaspoon of salt (or as desired)
- ½ a tablespoon of cumin powder
- ¼ teaspoon of turmeric powder
- ½ a bunch of green coriander, finely chopped
- 5 tablespoons of ghee or butter

DIRECTIONS

1. Whisk the eggs until intermixed.
2. Put the frying pan on the stove on medium heat and add the onion to the pan along with a tablespoon of water. Once all of the water evaporates, add the ghee.
3. When the onion becomes golden-colored, add the red chili and the garlic, and stir well. Then add the cumin, the turmeric and the salt and stir well on low heat.
4. Finally, add the eggs and stir continuously until the egg mixes with the rest of the ingredients. It is served with Arabic bread or Khameer bread.

LEVEL OF DIFFICULTY

DATE AND CHAMI - BREAKFAST

Main Dishes

Main dishes are usually served for lunch in my country, as it is considered the primary meal of the day in the Arab Gulf in general. As my mother told me that in the past, and due to the scarcity of resources, there was not much variety in the contents of meals. However, since my city, Dubai, is a coastal city, many of its residents worked in fishing, and so fish was their favorite meal. Back then people used to salt fish and store it in the summer to be consumed in the winter because it was not available then, either because it was in the reproduction phase or because of the weather conditions that prevented fishermen from going into the sea. Salted and dried fish is still popular and widely eaten nowadays even by the younger generations, it can actually be considered a delicacy of our cuisine. Locally, the salted fish is called "Al-Malih" (which literally means "The salty") , and various delicious dishes are prepared from it. As for the dried fish, it is called "Chseef". There is also another kind of small dried fish called "Jashie". Unfortunately, these types of dried and salted fish are probably not available in global markets and hence I didn't include recipes containing them in this book. However, I encourage anyone visiting my country to look for them in traditional restaurants and try them, they are really worth it !!

With the prosperity of commerce, tourism and the arrival of investors and immigrant workforce at my city, life has developed a lot, and the restaurants serving various types of meals diversified. Our local dishes were affected by adding some of the newcomer dishes to their list, such as Biryani, which comes from the Indian kitchen, as well as some types of bread, such as the Lebanese bread, the Indian bread and the Iranian bread. In addition, we were also impacted by the dishes of some Arabian countries, such as Egypt, Syria and Lebanon, like the dishes of stuffed vine leaves, Tabbouleh, Hummus, Kebbabs, and Kofta which became indispensable to us and are now regarded among the main dishes and prepared in most of our houses. Nevertheless, as is the case with the other parts of my book, in this section I am presenting our local authentic dishes as my mother used to prepare them.

Quzi (Rice and meat)

MAIN DISH

>> This dish is considered the main dish for feasts, weddings and festivities. In the past, it was exclusive for some people due to its expensiveness. But now, Quzi is mostly prepared in specialized traditional kitchens and usually a "tray" of Quzi costs between 1000 to 1500 AED depending on the origin and weight of the used meat.

My mother used to prepare it with the help of my father, due to his experience in making this dish, and aptly too, when guests visit us, or on occasions, and it was made with a complete sheep (the sheep used in Quzi is locally referred to as "Thubiha" which literary means the slaughtered animal). It is served with rice or Raqaq bread. Back then, cooking Quzi took so much time and effort as

4 hours PREP TIME

120 minutes COOKING

INGREDIENTS (First stage)

- Lamb thigh
- 100g of tamarind, soaked in 1 ¼ cup of water and strained from impurities (using a mesh strainer)
- 1 tablespoon of powdered turmeric
- 1 tablespoon of salt
- 1 tablespoon Bzaar (see page 149 for recipe)
- ½ tablespoon of powdered cinnamon
- ½ tablespoon of cardamom seeds
- ¼ tablespoon of clove
- ½ a teaspoon of saffron

DIRECTIONS

1. Mix the strained tamarind with all the other ingredients, season the thigh with them, and leave it marinate for two hours.
2. Put the seasoned thigh in a deep oven dish (Pyrex), and cover it well with aluminum foil.
3. Put the dish in the oven on 200°C for 1 ¼ hours then take it out.
4. Remove the aluminum foil and put the dish back in the oven on 150°C from the top side (i.e. Broil) for 10 minutes.

INGREDIENTS (Second stage)

- 2 cups of Indian Basmati rice, washed and soaked in water for 30 minutes
- 1 medium onion, chopped to small cubes
- 5 cardamom seeds
- 5 clove wholes
- 5 black pepper seeds
- 2 cinnamon sticks (wholes)
- 1 teaspoon of saffron soaked in a ¼ cup of rosewater
- 1 teaspoon of turmeric
- 1 tablespoon Bzaar (see page 149 for recipe)
- ¼ cup of vegetable oil
- 4 dried limes (see picture in page 144)
- 3 ½ cup of hot water

DIRECTIONS

1. Fry the onion in the oil in a pot on medium heat for 4 minutes.
2. Add the cardamom seeds, the clove, the black pepper seeds, the cinnamon sticks, the dried limes, the turmeric and the Bzaar.
3. Stir the mix for 2 minutes.
4. Add the rice and stir the mix, and after 2 minutes, pour the water and add the salt.
5. After 10 minutes, sprinkle the rice with the saffron rosewater.
6. Take the pot off the stove, cover it with aluminum foil and then with its own lid.
7. Put the pot back on the stove after putting a heat diffuser/ simmer ring between it and the low-heat flame for 15 minutes.

LEVEL OF DIFFICULTY

DATE AND CHAMI - MAIN DISHES

Third stage — INGREDIENTS (Al-Hashu: Filling)

- 1 cup of small chickpeas, washed and boiled with ½ teaspoon of salt for 12 minutes
- 4 onions, chopped to medium cubes
- 3 garlic cloves, finely chopped
- 3 tomatoes, chopped to medium cubes
- 1 cup of raisins
- 1 teaspoon of dried lemon powder
- 1 tablespoon of Bzaar (see page 149 for recipe)
- 1 teaspoon of powdered cinnamon
- ¼ teaspoon of clove
- 1 tablespoon of powdered cardamom
- ½ tablespoon of turmeric
- 2 potatoes, chopped to medium cubes, seasoned with salt and turmeric and fried
- 5 boiled eggs
- 1 teaspoon of saffron
- ⅓ cup of vegetable oil
- ¾ tablespoon of salt

DIRECTIONS

1. Fry the onion in the oil until it turns fair-colored.
2. Add the garlic to the onion and stir.
3. After 2 minutes, add the tomatoes and stir for 3 minutes.
4. Add the powdered lemon, the Bzaar, the cinnamon, the cardamom, the turmeric, the clove and the salt and stir the mix.
5. Add the raisins and the boiled chickpeas and stir for 3 minutes.
6. Add the fried potatoes and the saffron.
7. Leave it for 5 minutes on low heat.
8. Scoop the rice onto a large dish.
9. Put above it the cooked lamb thigh (from 1st stage).
10. Put Al-Hashu (filling) mixture around it and decorate it with the boiled eggs.
11. Serve it with yogurt salad.

Note

The type of rice affects the amount of water needed to cook it. Each cup of rice requires 2 or 1 ¾ cups of water.

Chili pepper can be added to the filling or the cooked meal. Many families in the past did not prefer the food with chili pepper, but now the general taste has changed, and it is sometimes added to the recipe.

Quozi can also be served with Raqaq bread, a traditional bread that is paper-thin, hence the name Raqaq, which could be translated as thin sheet.

Gubuli (Chicken)
MAIN DISH

>> This dish is regarded as one of the Arab Gulf dishes that are prepared in feasts and on various occasions. It is also prepared with meat.

First stage — INGREDIENTS (Chicken)

- 1 chicken (1 kg), washed and cut into 8 pieces
- 10 cardamom pods
- 10 black pepper seeds
- 10 clove wholes
- 3 cinnamon sticks
- 1 tablespoon of salt
- ½ teaspoon of powdered turmeric
- 50g of melted butter, with ½ teaspoon of ground saffron added to it
- ¼ teaspoon of powdered cardamom
- 3 liters of water to boil the chicken

DIRECTIONS

1. Boil the chicken in the 3 liters of water, adding the cardamom pods, black pepper, cinnamon and turmeric, simmer for 25 minutes.
2. Remove the chicken pieces from the pot. Put them in an oven dish (Pyrex), Spread the butter and saffron mixture, and sprinkle the ¼ teaspoon of cardamom powder on them.
3. Put them in the oven after at 180°C (ensure that the oven is pre-heated for at least 5 minutes).
4. Leave the chicken in the oven for 8 minutes.

Second stage — INGREDIENTS (Rice)

- 2 cups of Basmati rice, soaked in water for 15 minutes
- 3 ½ cups of chicken broth (the one resulting from boiling the chicken in the 1st stage)
- 4 tablespoons of vegetable oil
- 1 medium onion, finely chopped
- 4 dried limes (see picture in page 144)
- ½ tablespoon of powdered cardamom
- 1 tablespoon of salt (or as desired)
- 1 teaspoon of saffron, soaked in a ¼ cup of rosewater

LEVEL OF DIFFICULTY: ★★★

DIRECTIONS

1. Fry the onion in the oil in a pot until it becomes blonde-colored.
2. Add the cardamom and the lemon with stirring for a minute.
3. Add the rice after draining its water, and stir for 2 minutes (but carefully to avoid breaking the rice).
4. Add the chicken broth to the rice, add the salt and stir calmly.
5. Cover the pot and leave it on medium heat for 20 minutes.
6. Sprinkle the saffron rosewater on top of it.
7. Leave it for 8 minutes on low heat while putting a simmer ring against the direct flame under the pot.

The type of rice affects the amount of water necessary to cook it. So in the beginning, just use 3 cups of chicken broth. After 20 minutes, take some of the rice to make sure it is cooked. Here you will know whether it needs more broth or not.

Third stage — INGREDIENTS *(Decoration mix)*

- 2 medium onions, chopped to medium slices
- 1 large carrot, cut to 3cm thick slices and seasoned with salt and turmeric
- 2 large potatoes, cut to 3cm thick slices and seasoned with salt and turmeric
- ¼ cup of cashew nuts
- ½ cup of raisins
- 1 tablespoon of Bzaar (see page for recipe)
- ½ teaspoon of powdered cinnamon
- 1 teaspoon of saffron
- ¼ teaspoon of powdered clove
- 1 tablespoon of salt
- ¼ cup of ghee
- ¼ tablespoon of powdered cardamom

DIRECTIONS

1. Fry the carrot and potato slices in the ghee and set them aside.
2. Fry the cashew nuts (until they become blonde-colored) and set them aside.
3. In the same pan and in the remaining ghee, fry the onion until it becomes golden-colored.
4. Add the raisins and keep stirring for two minutes.
5. Add the spices, the cinnamon, the clove, the saffron, the cardamom and the salt.
6. Stir the mix and put them on low heat for 3 minutes.
7. Scoop the rice in a large dish.
8. Put the decoration mix (the onion, raisins and spices mix) and then the chicken.
9. Decorate them with the fried cashew nuts, fried potatoes and fried carrots.

Machboos Chicken

MAIN DISH

>> This dish is prepared in most Arab Gulf countries and it can be prepared with fish, meat or chicken. It is one of the traditional and ancient dishes in my country, and this is how my mother used to make it.

INGREDIENTS

- 1 Chicken (1 kg), cut into 4 pieces
- 2 cups of basmati rice, soaked in water for 15 minutes and then drained of water
- 3 onions, chopped to medium cubes
- 5 garlic cloves shredded
- 3 tomatoes, chopped to small cubes
- 2 chili red peppers
- 1 tablespoon of powdered cardamom
- 1 tablespoon of Bzaar (see page 149 for recipe)
- ½ tablespoon of cumin
- 1 ½ tablespoon of salt
- 1 teaspoon of cinnamon
- ½ teaspoon of saffron soaked in a ¼ cup of rosewater
- 2 potatoes, chopped to medium cubes
- 3 dried limes (see picture in page 144)
- ¼ cup of vegetable oil
- 4 cups of boiling water
- 3 tablespoons of vegetable oil

DIRECTIONS

1. Season the chicken with half of the above-mentioned spices (except the salt, just use ¼ tablespoon for this step).
2. Fry the onion in a pot in the ¼ cup of oil on medium heat until it withers and starts to turn blonde-colored.
3. Add the garlic and stir for two minutes.
4. Add the tomatoes, the rest of the spices, the salt and the dried limes with stirring.
5. Add the chicken and stir it with the rest of the ingredients for 3 minutes.
6. Pour the boiling water on the mixture, and leave it on medium heat for 20 minutes.
7. Remove the chicken pieces from the pot and set them aside.
8. Add the potatoes, and after 5 minutes, add the rice and cover the pot for 20 minutes (still on medium heat).
9. Sprinkle the rice with the saffron rosewater and turn down the heat to low.
10. Fry the chicken in the 3 tablespoons of oil (in a separate pan).
11. Put the fried chicken pieces on top of the rice in the pot.
12. Cover the pot tightly and keep it on low heat for additional 5 minutes (with a simmer ring under the pot).
13. Scoop the rice on the serving dish and put the chicken pieces on top of the rice. Serve it with yogurt salad (recipe in page 101).

Meat saloonah (stew) with Bobar (pumpkin)

MAIN DISH

>> *This dish is delicious and easy to make, we eat it with plain rice or bread, and it may be made with fish, chicken or just vegetables. My mother used to make it with tamarind as in the following recipe.*

INGREDIENTS

- 700g of lamb meat with or without the bones (preferred with the bones for more delicious taste)
- 2 onions, chopped to medium cubes
- 5 garlic cloves, finely chopped
- A pumpkin (300g) chopped to medium cubes
- 2 potatoes, chopped to medium cubes
- 4 tomatoes, cut into quarters
- ½ a bunch of coriander, finely chopped
- 2 green peppers, chopped (without the seeds)
- 70g of tomato paste
- 100g of tamarind, soaked in a cup of water and strained using a mesh strainer (the resulting juice is what will be used in this recipe)
- ¼ cup of vegetable oil.

SPICES

- 1 tablespoon of 7-spices or any Arabian spices
- 1 teaspoon of powdered cardamom
- ½ tablespoon of powdered turmeric
- ½ tablespoon of powdered cumin
- ½ teaspoon of powdered cinnamon
- ¼ teaspoon of powdered clove
- ¾ tablespoons of salt (or as desired)
- 6 cups of hot water

DIRECTIONS

1. Fry the onion in the oil until it withers.
2. Add the garlic and stir them for 1 minute.
3. Add the meat and stir for 3 minutes
4. Add the pepper and the tomatoes and stir for 3 minutes.
5. Add the tomato paste and all the spices except the clove, add the tamarind juice, and stir the mixture.
6. Add the boiling water, and after 25 minutes, add the potatoes, the pumpkin and the salt, and cover the pot for 15 minutes.
7. Add the powdered clove after you make sure the meat is cooked.
8. Taste the mixture to check the saltiness and add some salt as desired if necessary, then leave it on low heat for 5 minutes.
9. Pour the Saloona in the serving container and serve it with saffron rice or plain rice.

Adding the clove in the beginning gives the food an undesired dark color. This is what my mother taught me and so I tend to add the cloves towards the end.

Fish Tahtah

MAIN DISH

30+60 minutes
PREP TIME + COOKING

> This dish is also one of our traditional dishes. My mother used to make it for us with tuna fish, however, I decided to use sea bass in the following recipe. The naming of the dish comes from the fact that the fish and the other ingredients are put in the bottom of the pot while the rice is put on top as Taht (with sharp H) in Arabic means below.

 ## Onion Mixture

INGREDIENTS

- 2 medium onions, cut into medium cubes
- 6 garlic cloves, shredded
- 5 tablespoons of ghee
- ½ a bunch of coriander, finely chopped
- 3 tablespoons of dill, finely chopped
- 1 tablespoon of Bzaar (see page 149 for recipe)
- 3 tomatoes, cut into medium cubes
- 1 teaspoon of salt (or as desired)
- ¼ tablespoon of powdered turmeric
- ½ tablespoon of powdered cumin
- 1 teaspoon of powdered dried lime
- ¼ teaspoon of powdered clove
- ½ tablespoon of powdered coriander

DIRECTIONS

1. Put a pan on medium heat, put the onions and the 5 tablespoons of ghee in it and stir.
2. After 2 minutes, add the garlic and the dried lime powder.
3. After 1 minute, add the tomatoes and stir until it is cooked and becomes mixed with the onion and the garlic (around 4 minutes).
4. Add all the spices and the salt and stir the mixture.
5. After 1 minute, add the fresh coriander and dill. Keep it on low heat for further 2 minutes. Set aside this onion mixture.

 ## Fish

INGREDIENTS

- 2 sea basses, each cut in half
- 5 garlic cloves
- 1 teaspoon of salt
- 1 teaspoon of powdered turmeric
- 1 tablespoon of Bzaar (see page 149 for recipe)
- ½ teaspoon of powdered cumin
- ½ tablespoon of powdered coriander
- 1 cup of vegetable oil
- 1 lemon, cut into 2 halves

SEASONING THE FISH

1. Cut each fish in half, rub it with lemon and wash it well
2. Put them in a somewhat deep container
3. Put all the above-mentioned ingredient in a mortar and grind them well with the pestle until they become like paste.
4. Smother the fish pieces with the seasoning paste.
5. Cover the container well and keep it aside for an hour for the fish to marinate.
6. Fry the fish well in the oil and set it aside.

DATE AND CHAMI - MAIN DISHES

INGREDIENTS — *Rice*

- 2 cups of basmati rice, washed and soaked in water for 15 minutes
- 2 medium onions, chopped to medium cubes
- 3 tomatoes, chopped to medium cubes
- 5 cloves of garlic, shredded
- 3 ½ liters of water
- 1 teaspoon of cumin wholes
- 1 ½ tablespoons of salt
- 3 cinnamon sticks
- 5 clove wholes
- 5 cardamom seeds
- 2 tablespoons of ghee

DIRECTIONS

1. Put the water in a pot on the stove and add the cumin wholes, the cinnamon sticks, the clove wholes and the salt.
2. When the water boils, add the rice after draining it of the soaking water, and stir it for a little while.
3. After 6 minutes, drain the rice of the water and leave it aside in the colander.
4. In the same pot, put half the onion mixture in the bottom of the pot.
5. Put the fish on top of it.
6. Add the remaining half of the onion mixture on top of the fish.
7. Put the boiled rice on the mixture and the fish (Level the surface of the rice with a spoon).
8. Sprinkle the surface of the rice with the ghee.
9. Put it on low heat for 10 minutes, with a simmer ring under the pot.
10. Scoop the rice in the serving plate. Put the fish and the mixture on top of it.
11. Serve it with onion, arugula and tomato salad (see page 97 for recipe).

Note: The types of fish that are mostly available worldwide and suitable for this dish, from my experience, are the sea bass and seabream. However, in my country we use other fish that is known across the Arab Gulf.

Madhrouba

MAIN DISH

» Madhrouba is a delicious Arab Gulf dish that is made with meat, chicken or even fish. Sometimes, my mother made it for us with tuna fish and so this the one I chose to include in this book. The dish is called Madhrouba (battered or beaten) because after preparing it, it is beaten with a large wooden spoon to mix the ingredients well.

INGREDIENTS

- 500g Egyptian rice
- 500g boneless tuna fish fillets
- 3 onions, finely chopped to cubes
- 5 tomatoes, finely chopped to cubes
- 5 cloves of garlic, shredded
- ⅓ cup of ghee
- 1 tablespoon of Bzaar (see page 149 for recipe)
- 1 tablespoon of powdered cumin
- 1 tablespoon of powdered coriander
- ½ tablespoon of powdered turmeric
- 1 tablespoon of powdered dried lime
- 70g of tomato paste
- ½ tablespoon of powdered cinnamon
- ¼ tablespoon of powdered clove
- ¼ tablespoon of powdered chili pepper
- 1 pack of fresh coriander, finely chopped
- ½ a pack of dill, finely chopped
- 1 ½ tablespoon of salt (or as desired)
- 1 medium onion, cut to thin slices
- 4 tablespoons of ghee
- juice of 1 lemon
- ½ teaspoon of salt
- 4 cups of boiling water

DIRECTIONS

1. Clean the fish well, season it with the lemon juice and ½ a teaspoon of salt, and set it aside for 10 minutes.
2. Put the chopped onion with the 1/3 cup of ghee in a pot of suitable size and fry it on medium heat for 3 minutes.
3. Add the garlic and stir for a minute.
4. Add the fish and stir for 2 minutes.
5. Add the tomatoes and the spices one by one and stir for 3 minutes.
6. Add the tomato paste and the salt and stir for 2 minutes.
7. Add the washed rice and stir the mixture for a minute.
8. Pour the boiling water and stir thoroughly.
9. Turn the stove off and make sure the saltiness is adequate.
10. Cover the pot with aluminum foil in addition to its own lid.
11. Put it in the oven for 20 minutes on 180°C temperature.
12. Take the pot out of the oven and use a handheld electric blender. Put it on low heat for another 5 minutes.
13. To serve, fry the sliced onion in the 4 tablespoons of ghee.
14. Scoop the Madhroba in the serving dish and decorate it with the fried onion along with the ghee in which it was fried.

Shrimp Momawash

MAIN DISH

» *It is a famous dish in some Arab Gulf countries, particularly in Kuwait. My mother used to make it for us, and this is her recipe for making it.*

INGREDIENTS

- 1 cup of fresh shrimp, stripped of the peel and washed thoroughly
- 2 ½ cup of basmati rice, washed and soaked in the water for 15 minutes
- 1 cup of brown lentil, washed
- 3 onions, finely chopped
- 1 large tomato, chopped to medium cubes
- 6 cloves of garlic, grounded
- ½ a pack of fresh coriander, finely chopped
- 3 red chili peppers, finely chopped after removing the seeds
- 4 cups of hot water
- ¼ cup of vegetable oil
- 2 dried limes
- 1 teaspoon of powdered cardamom
- 1 teaspoon of powdered cumin
- 1 teaspoon of powdered coriander
- 1 teaspoon of Bzaar (see page 149 for recipe)
- 1 ¼ tablespoon of salt (or as desired)

DIRECTIONS

1. Put the ghee in a pot on medium heat.
2. Add the onion and stir for 3 minutes.
3. Add the garlic and stir for 2 minutes.
4. Add the shrimp and stir for 2 minutes.
5. Add the pepper and the tomatoes and stir for 2 minutes.
6. Add all the spices and the salt and stir for a minute.
7. Add the dried limes and the lentil.
8. Add 2 cups of hot water and leave it for 10 minutes on medium heat.
9. Add the rice and the fresh coriander and stir for a little while.
10. Add the remaining hot water and stir calmly.
11. Cover the pot tightly and keep it on medium heat for 25 minutes.
12. Put the simmer ring and put the pot on it on low heat for 8 minutes.
13. Scoop in the serving dish and serve it with Daqqus (recipe in page 151)

DATE AND CHAMI - MAIN DISHES

Matfi Samak

MAIN DISH

>> This dish is delicious and my daughters love it. When tuna, seabream, or seabass is available in the house, they always ask me to make it, and they prefer to eat it with sweet rice.

INGREDIENTS

- 3 sea basses, whole or cut in halves
- 2 medium onions, finely chopped
- 2 tomatoes, peeled and finely chopped
- 4 cloves of garlic, shredded or grounded
- 2 tablespoons of ginger, fresh and shredded
- 3 green chili peppers, with the seeds removed
- ½ pack of coriander, finely chopped
- ¼ pack of dill, finely chopped
- 3 dried limes, pierced but not opened
- ½ red peppers, finely chopped
- 70g of tomato paste
- 1 cup of vegetable oil (to fry the fish)
- ½ tablespoon of powdered cumin
- ½ tablespoon of powdered coriander
- ½ tablespoon of Bzaar (see page 149 for recipe)
- 1 teaspoon of salt (or as desired)
- 40g of tamarind soacked for 5 minutes in 1 cup of warm water, and the strained with a mesh strainer (the resultant tamarind juice is what is used in this recipe)

FISH SEASONING

- 5 cloves of garlic
- Juice of 2 limes
- ½ tablespoon of Bzaar (see page 149 for recipe)
- ¼ tablespoon of powdered turmeric
- ¼ tablespoon of powdered coriander
- ¼ tablespoon of powdered cumin
- ¾ teaspoon of salt

SEASONING RECIPE

1. Put the seasoning ingredients in a mortar and grind them with the pestle until they become coherent like paste.
2. Clean the fish thoroughly of gills, fins and peel (if any, depending on the type of fish).
3. Smother the fish with the seasoning paste.
4. Leave it marinate for 30 minutes.

DIRECTIONS

1. Put a pan on the stove.
2. Pour a cup of oil in it and fry the fish.
3. Filter the remaining frying oil of impurities.
4. Put the oil back in the pan.
5. Put the onion and fry it until it starts to turn fair-colored.
6. Add the garlic, the ginger and the green chili pepper, and stir for 2 minutes (on medium heat).
7. Add the tomato paste, all the spices and the dried limes and stir for 2 minutes.
8. Add the tomatoes, the fresh coriander and the dill and stir for a minute.
9. Add the tamarind juice and stir for a little while.
10. After leaving the mixture for 5 minutes on medium heat, add the fish to the pan.
11. Leave it for 15 minutes on low heat.
12. Serve it with plain rice or sweet rice (see page 78 for recipe).

DATE AND CHAMI - MAIN DISHES

My Mother's Macaroni

MAIN DISH

>> Although Macaroni or Pasta is not among our traditional dishes, my mother used to prepare it in her own way, and I used to help her prepare the ingredients. When a macaroni factory was established in Dubai in 1979, macaroni became widespread here, but imported macaroni was available in our markets years before that and that was what inspired my mother to prepare this dish in the early-mid 1970s.

 **INGREDIENTS**

- 500g of macaroni (of the type you prefer)
- 300g of minced beef
- 3 onions, chopped to medium cubes
- 1 large carrot, chopped to medium cubes and fried
- 1 large potato, chopped to medium cubes and fried to the color gold
- 3 cloves of garlic, ground
- Green bell pepper, chopped to medium cubes.
- ½ pack of coriander, finely chopped
- ¼ cup of olive oil
- 70g of tomato paste
- ½ tablespoon of Arabian spices or 7-spices
- ¼ tablespoon of powdered turmeric
- ½ tablespoon of cardamom
- ¼ tablespoon of cinnamon
- ½ tablespoon of salt (or as desired)
- Juice of 1 lemon
- 2 liters of water (to boil the macaroni)
- 1 tablespoon of salt (to boil the macaroni)
- 3 tablespoons of vegetable oil

 **DIRECTIONS**

1. Boil the macaroni in the 2 liters of water and the tablespoon of salt for 14 minutes.
2. Drain the macaroni of the boiling water and set it aside covered to maintain its softness.
3. In the same pot, put the olive oil on medium heat.
4. Add the onion and stir for 3 minutes.
5. Add the ground beef and stir for 4 minutes.
6. Add the green bell pepper and stir for 2 minutes.
7. Add the spices and the salt one by one and stir continuously for 2 minutes.
8. Add the tomato paste and the coriander and stir the mix for 2 minutes.
9. Add the fried potatoes and carrot, and stir the mix for a minute.
10. Add the macaroni and the lemon juice. Stir the mix and check the saltiness (add more salt, if desired).
11. Put in the serving dish and serve.

 *Note* — *Some people prefer to eat this Macaroni with the spicy Daqqus sauce (recipe in page 151).*

Ursiya

MAIN DISH

» Ursiya is commonly eaten it in Rmadan for the Suhur (late night meal) or Iftar (fast breaking meal) in Ramadan as it provides the body with energy and makes it able to endure the hours of fasting throughout the day. It is also eaten throughout the year as lunch or dinner.

 **INGREDIENTS**

- 2 cups of jasmine rice, washed and soaked in water for 15 minutes
- 630g of chicken breasts, cut to small pieces
- 1 teaspoon of powdered cardamom
- ½ tablespoon of white pepper
- 5 cups of water
- 1 ¼ tablespoons of salt
- 4 tablespoons of ghee

15+60 minutes
PREP TIME + COOKING

 **DIRECTIONS**

1. After draining the rice, put it and all the other ingredients, except the ghee, in a pressure cooker.
2. Set the timer to 30 minutes (or Congee settings, if available).
3. After the 30 minutes pass, open the cooker to make sure the Ursiya is cooked. The Ursiya is cooked when its structure is like that of porridge.
4. Scoop it in the serving dish, level it with cow ghee and serve it.

Note

Recently, I have been using Amazon-brand electric pressure cooker in making it and the resultant Ursiya is just as good as the one prepared in the traditional way of beating.

LEVEL OF DIFFICULTY

DATE AND CHAMI - MAIN DISHES   57

Lamb Liver Hamsa

MAIN DISH

>> My mother used to cook lamb liver in different ways, including grilling and frying. The method I presented here is called Hamsa, which is somewhat similar to stir-fry.

INGREDIENTS

- 500g of lamb liver, cut to long strips
- 3 medium onions, cut to slices
- 4 cloves of garlic, cut to thin slices
- 3 tomatoes, cut to thin slices
- 3 green peppers
- 1 tablespoon of tomato paste
- 3 tablespoons of butter
- 3 tablespoons of olive oil
- ½ pack of coriander, finely chopped
- ½ tablespoon of powdered cumin
- ½ tablespoon of powdered coriander
- ¼ tablespoon of powdered turmeric
- ½ tablespoon of salt (or as desired)
- ½ tablespoon of powdered cardamom
- 1 teaspoon of saffron
- 4 tablespoons of hot water

DIRECTIONS

1. Put the liver in a pot on medium heat and cook it until it becomes dry (until the liquid produced from it evaporates).
2. Add the butter and the oil, and stir the liver with them for 4 minutes.
3. Add the onion and stir for 3 minutes.
4. Add the garlic and stir for a minute.
5. Add the tomatoes and the spices and stir continuously for 3 minutes.
6. Add the green pepper and tomato paste and stir for 2 minutes.
7. Add the salt, the saffron and the 4 tablespoons of water with stirring on low heat.
8. After 5 minutes, the liver will have been cooked.
9. Serve it with Arabian bread.

Aesh bil Zefraan (Saffron Rice)

MAIN DISH — *Vegetarian*

> This type of rice is usually served with grilled chicken or grilled meat.

 **INGREDIENTS**

- 2 cups of basmati rice, washed and soaked for 20 minutes in warm water
- 1 teaspoon of saffron
- ¼ cup of rosewater
- ½ teaspoon of powdered cardamom
- 6 cups of water
- 1 ½ tablespoon of salt
- 4 tablespoons of cow ghee or vegetable oil

DIRECTIONS

1. Soak the saffron in rose water for 10 minutes before cooking the rice.
2. Put the water and the salt in a pot on medium heat.
3. When the water boils, put the rice after draining it of the soaking water.
4. After 6 minutes, drain the rice of the cooking water.
5. Put the rice back into the pot and sprinkle it with the saffron rosewater first and then with the powdered cardamom.
6. Finally, sprinkle the ghee or the oil on the rice.
7. Close the pot tightly (with its lid), put the simmer ring under the pot on low heat for 5-8 minutes i.e. until steam starts rising from it.
8. Scoop it and serve it with meat, chicken or vegetables.

Vegetable Hamsa

MAIN DISH — *Vegetarian*

>> *My mother used to make us this dish for dinner.*

INGREDIENTS

- 2 potatoes, chopped to medium cubes
- 1 large eggplant, chopped to medium cubes, sprinkled with some salt and kept for 3 minutes, then washed and dried
- 300g of pumpkin, chopped to medium cubes
- 2 carrots, chopped to medium cubes
- 1 onion, finely chopped
- 4 cloves of garlic, shredded
- Green bell pepper, chopped to medium cubes
- 4 large and red tomatoes, finely chopped after removing the peel
- 70g of tomato paste
- ½ tablespoon of cumin
- 1 tablespoon of fresh mint
- 3 tablespoons of dill
- ½ tablespoon of Bzaar (see page 149 for recipe)
- ¾ tablespoon of salt (or as desired)
- ¼ cup of hot water
- ¼ cup of olive oil
- 1 ½ cup of vegetable oil (for frying)

DIRECTIONS

1. In a pan, fry the vegetables as follows:
    a. The potatoes for 5 minutes, and set it aside.
    b. The carrots for 3 minutes, and set it aside.
    c. The pumpkin for 3 minutes, and set it aside.
    d. The eggplant for 3 minutes, and set it aside.
2. Put a pot on medium heat and put the olive oil in it.
3. Put the onion in the pot and stir it for 3 minutes.
4. Add the garlic and the green bell pepper and stir for 2 minutes.
5. Add the cumin and the Bzaar and stir for a minute.
6. Add the fresh tomatoes and the tomato paste and stir for 2 minutes.
7. Pour the water and the salt, stir them, and leave them for 2 minutes.
8. Add the fried vegetables and stir calmly for 5 minutes (on low heat).
9. Add the dill and the mint.
10. Leave the pot on low heat with the lid tightly closed for 10 minutes.
11. Serve with bread.

Note: *Sprinkling the eggplant with salt before rinsing it with water and drying it reduces its absorption of oil when frying it.*

Shrimp Hamsa

MAIN DISH

» This dish is one of the delicious seafood dishes. Here in the Arab Gulf, we prepare it in different ways, whether with the rice like Murabyan, grilled as a side dish, or as Hamsa (similar to stir-fry) or Saloona (similar to stew).

 **INGREDIENTS**

- 700g of fresh shrimp, peeled and thoroughly cleaned
- 2 onions, cut to long strips
- 4 cloves of garlic, shredded
- 1 tablespoon of fresh ginger, shredded
- 1 pack of coriander, finely chopped
- 70g of tomato paste
- 1 teaspoon of salt (or as desired)
- 1 tablespoon of powdered coriander
- ½ tablespoon of powdered cumin
- 1 teaspoon of Arabian spices
- ½ teaspoon of saffron
- 5 tablespoons of olive oil
- Juice of 1 lemon
- ½ teaspoon of red chili pepper
- 3 tablespoons of hot water

 **DIRECTIONS**

1. Put the onion in a pan on medium heat and add the olive oil.
2. After 4 minutes, add the garlic and the ginger and stir for 2 minutes.
3. Add the shrimp and stir well for 4 minutes.
4. Turn down the heat to low.
5. Add the spices and the powdered cumin, coriander and red chili and stir for 2 minutes.
6. Add the tomato paste, the salt and the hot water and stir for 3 minutes.
7. Add the fresh coriander and the lemon and keep the pan covered for 3 minutes.
8. Serve with onion rice (recipe in page 75) or Arabian bread, whichever is desired.

Marqooga

MAIN DISH

>> Marqooqa is a traditional and delicious Arab Gulf dish that can be made with meat, chicken or vegetables.

INGREDIENTS

- 500g lamb meat with or without the bones, cut to medium pieces
- 2 cups of white plain flour
- 2 onions, chopped to medium cubes
- 2 large tomatoes, cut into quarters
- 1 large potato, chopped to medium cubes
- 2 carrots, chopped to medium cubes
- ½ medium pumpkin, cut to medium cubes
- ¼ pack of coriander, averagely chopped
- 6 cloves of garlic, grounded
- 1 tablespoon of shredded ginger
- 70g of tomato paste
- 1 tablespoon Bzaar (see page 149 for recipe)
- ½ tablespoon of powdered cumin
- ½ tablespoon of powdered coriander
- ½ teaspoon of powdered cinnamon
- ¼ teaspoon of powdered clove
- ½ teaspoon of cardamom
- 5 tablespoons of vegetable oil
- ½ teaspoon of powdered red chili (or as desired)
- 1 ¼ tablespoons of salt (or as desired)
- 2 tablespoons of vegetable oil (for the dough)
- ¼ tablespoon of salt (for the dough)
- ¼ cup of water (for the dough)
- 5 ½ cups of hot water

DIRECTIONS

1. Knead the flour, the 2 tablespoons of vegetable oil and the ¼ tablespoon of salt in a mixer or by hand.
2. Add the water gradually while kneading.
3. After 5 minutes of kneading, divide the dough into walnut-sized balls and then stretch them to disks (with a diameter of 8cm and a thickness of 0.5 cm).
4. Set the disks aside and keep them separated in order not to stick to one another.
5. Put a pot on the stove on medium heat, add the onion, and then add the oil and stir for 3 minutes.
6. Add the garlic and the ginger to the pot and stir for a minute.
7. Add the lamb meat, then the Bzaar, the cumin, the coriander, the cardamom, the red chili, the cinnamon and the 1 tablespoon of salt and stir for 4 minutes until the meat absorbs the spices and becomes mixed with them.
8. Add the tomato paste and stir for a minute.
9. Add the vegetables and the tomatoes and stir the mixture for 2 more minutes.
10. Add the water and stir for a little while, then leave the pot on medium heat for 25 to 30 minutes.
11. Add the disks to the mixture in the pot as follows: drop one disk in, move it with the spoon, then drop the other and use the spoon to keep them apart, and so on until all the disks are put. For 5 minutes, keep moving the spoon amidst them so as not to stick to one another.
12. Cover the pot and leave it on low heat for 20 minutes.

Herees

MAIN DISH

>> Harees is eaten it a lot in Ramadan, on feasts and on various occasions. It is one of the main dishes in the Arab Gulf countries and it is a quite satisfying and filing dish. Traditionally, Harees is cooked on embers and beaten with a large wooden bat for it to gain coherence. However, for the sake of simplicity, I used an electric pressure cooker and an electric hand blender for the recipe in this book.

INGREDIENTS

- 500g of Pearl Barley, soaked for 6 hours
- 500g of lamb tenderloin, washed thoroughly
- 1 ¼ tablespoon of salt (as desired)
- 1 ¼ liters of water
- 4 tablespoons of ghee

DIRECTIONS

1. Drain the barley of the soaking water.
2. Put the barley, the meat, the water and the salt in an electric pressure cooker.
3. Leave it for an hour.
4. Mix the Harees well with an electric hand mixer.
5. Leave it for 15 to 20 minutes in the heating mode of the electric pressure cooker.
6. Scoop it in a serving dish and spread ghee on it.

Sprinkling the eggplant with salt before rinsing it with water and drying it reduces its absorption of oil when frying it.

Fish Saloona (stew) with Merees

MAIN DISH

>> This dish is one of the ancient and traditional dishes. It is a fish dish but it is prepared with date infusion (locally called Marees). It has a special taste combining the sweetness of dates, the sourness of lemon and a hint of saltiness.

INGREDIENTS

- 5 fillets of tuna fish, cleaned and seasoned with ½ tablespoon Bzaar, juice of 1 lemon and sprinkles of salt and left to marinate for 1 hour
- 3 medium onions, chopped to small cubes
- 2 large tomatoes, finely chopped
- 5 cloves of garlic, shredded
- 2 green peppers, chopped after removing the seeds
- ½ bunch of coriander, finely chopped
- 1 cup of date fruits, soaked in 2 cups of warm water for 30 minutes
- 1 tablespoon of Bzaar (see page 149 for recipe)
- ½ tablespoon of powdered cumin
- ¾ tablespoon of powdered coriander
- ¼ teaspoon of powdered red chili
- ¾ tablespoon of salt
- 3 dried limes, pierced
- 70g of tomato paste
- 5 cardamom seeds
- 4 clove wholes
- 2 cinnamon sticks
- ½ cup of hot water
- ⅓ cup of corn oil

DIRECTIONS

1. Put a deep pan or a pot on medium heat. Pour the oil in it, and a minute later, add the onion and stir for 2 minutes.
2. Add the garlic, the green pepper, the cardamom seeds, the clove wholes and the cinnamon sticks.
3. Stir the mixture for 3 minutes.
4. Put the fish slices and leave them for 2 minutes.
5. Flip the fish slices on the other side.
6. After 1 minute, add the Bzaar, the cumin, the red chili, the salt and the dry lemons.
7. Add the date infusion (Marees), and move the fish calmly so as not to break it.
8. Add the tomato paste and the hot water.
9. Leave it for 20 minutes on medium heat.
10. Add the coriander, and turn down the heat to low, after 6 minutes, turn off the stove.
11. Serve with onion rice (recipe in page 75).

Semach Mashwai (Grilled Fish)

MAIN DISH

» My mother preferred to grill the fish in the furnace and on charcoal, and she did not prefer the modern ways of grilling. Nevertheless, I find fish grilled in the oven a reasonable alternative when a furnace or a BBQ are not available.

INGREDIENTS

- 3 seabream fishes, sea basses or whatever type of fish you prefer
- 3 onions, cut to slices
- 3 lemons, cut to slices
- 6 cloves of garlic, cut to slices
- Juice of 2 lemons
- 2 tablespoons of salt
- 1 ½ tablespoons of Bzaar

DIRECTIONS

1. Clean the fish properly and make slanted cuts in its surface.
2. Mix the onion, lemon slices and garlic slices with ½ teaspoon of Bzaar.
3. Season the fish with the remaining Bzaar and the 2 tablespoons of salt from the inside and the outside, and the set it aside to marinate for 30 minutes.
4. Preheat the oven on 180°C temperature for about 20 minutes.
5. Stuff the incisions in the fish with the onion, garlic and lemon mixture (from step 2), and stuff the inside of the fish with them as well.
6. Spread little bit of oil in a baking dish/ oven tray, put the fish in it and put it in the preheated oven on 180°C temperature.
7. After 30 minutes, the fish should be grilled.
8. Serve with onion rice (recipe in page 75), salad and Daqqus (recipe in page 151).

Note: If the fish is small, the grilling duration decreases to 20 minutes, and 15 minutes in case of fish slices or fillets. However, for larger fish, the grilling duration of around 40-45 minutes should be sufficient.

Aesh bil Bessal (Onion Rice)

MAIN DISH — Vegetarian

74 DATE AND CHAMI - MAIN DISHES

INGREDIENTS

- 2 cups of basmati rice, washed and soaked for 20 minutes in warm water
- 3 medium onions, cut to slices
- 6 cups of water
- 1 ½ tablespoon of salt
- 4 tablespoons of cow ghee or vegetable oil

DIRECTIONS

1. Put the water and the salt in a pot on medium heat.
2. When the water boils, put the rice after draining it of the soaking water.
3. After 6 minutes, drain the rice of the boiling water.
4. Leave the rice in the colander.
5. After the rice-boiling pot dries, put the cow ghee or the oil in it.
6. Add the onion and stir until it becomes brown-colored.
7. Take half the onion/ ghee mix and mix it with the rice in the colander, and set the other half aside.
8. Put the rice back into the pot, cover the pot tightly and put it on medium heat with the simmer ring under it for 10 minutes until the steam starts rising from it.
9. Put the rice it in the serving dish and decorate it with the remaining fried onion/ghee mix.
10. Serve it with grilled fish, fried fish, chicken or vegetables.

Chicken Yriesh
(Groats) — MAIN DISH

INGREDIENTS

- 1 ½ cups of groats, soaked in water for an hour and then drained
- ¾ cups of Egyptian rice, soaked in water for 30 minutes and drained
- 800g of chicken breasts, chopped to small cubes
- 1 cup of yogurt
- 2 tablespoons of ghee
- ½ tablespoon of powdered cumin
- ¼ tablespoon of cardamom
- 1 teaspoon of Bzaar
- 1 ½ tablespoons of salt (or as desired)
- 3 ½ cups of warm water

DIRECTIONS

1. Put all the above-mentioned ingredients, except the yogurt, in an electric pressure cooker.
2. Leave them for 50 minutes.
3. After the all steam comes out, open the cooker.
4. Add the yogurt, stir the Yriesh and leave it for 15 minutes in the heating mode of the electric pressure cooker.
5. Mix it with an electric hand blender.
6. Scoop it in the serving dish and decorate it with Kashna.

INGREDIENTS — Kashna

- 1 large onion, finely chopped
- 1 teaspoon of powdered dry lemon
- 1 teaspoon of powdered cumin
- 1 teaspoon of Bzaar
- ½ teaspoon of powdered red chili
- ½ teaspoon of salt (or as desired)
- 5 tablespoons of cow ghee

DIRECTIONS

1. Put the onion and the ghee in a pot on medium heat.
2. Fry the onion until it becomes golden-colored.
3. Reduce the heat to low and add all the remaining ingredients.
4. Stir the mixture well for 2 minutes.
5. Decorate the Yriesh with it.

Note: *Kashna means onion and spices mixture.*

Muhammar (Sweet Rice)

MAIN DISH — Vegetarian

>> This rice is from our heritage, and it is prepared in two ways: either with dates (called Barany-ush) or with sugar (called Muhammar). It is served with fried fish, Matfi or as desired.

INGREDIENTS

- 2 cups of basmati rice, washed and soaked in water for 30 minutes
- 1 ¼ cups of sugar
- 8 cardamom seeds
- 8 black pepper wholes
- 1 cinnamon stick
- 4 cups of hot water
- 4 tablespoons of ghee or vegetable oil (as desired)
- 1 average onion, finely chopped

DIRECTIONS

1. Put the pot on medium heat.
2. Put the sugar in and let it caramelize (watch it carefully so as not to let it burn).
3. Add the hot water (and be careful of splashes).
4. When the caramelized sugar dissolves, add the cardamom, the black pepper and the cinnamon.
5. When the sugar water boils, add the rice and stir for a little while.
6. Cover the pot and leave it on medium heat until the water dries completely. Then turn off the heat.
7. In a pan, fry the onion until it becomes blonde-colored, and then sprinkle it on the rice.
8. Put the pot back on heat with a simmer ring for 10 minutes.
9. Before serving it, mix it and then scoop it in the serving dish beside the fish.

Images from old and rural Dubai

Soups & Salads

Lentil Soup

SOUPS & SALADS

Vegetarian

> My mother used to make Lentil soup for us in the winter, as it brings us warmth and has a distinctive taste.

INGREDIENTS

- 250g of lentil
- 4 tablespoons of butter or vegetable oil
- 5 cloves of garlic, chopped to slices
- 2 medium onions, finely chopped
- 3 tomatoes, chopped to small cubes
- 1 tablespoon of powdered cumin
- 1 tablespoon of powdered coriander
- 1 teaspoon of cumin seeds
- 1 teaspoon of powdered turmeric
- 1 liter of chicken broth
- Juice of 1 lemon
- 1 tablespoon of salt (as desired)
- 1 pack of fresh coriander
- Lemon slices

25+30 minutes
PREP TIME + COOKING

DIRECTIONS

1. Fry the onion on medium heat for 3 minutes.
2. Add the cumin seeds and the garlic, and after 2 minutes, add the tomatoes.
3. After 2 minutes, add the powdered coriander, cumin and turmeric and stir for a minute.
4. Add the lentil and stir everything for 3 minutes to mix them together.
5. Pour the chicken broth and stir the contents well.
6. Leave them on low heat for 15 minutes.
7. Add the coriander and the lemon juice and cover the pot for 10 minutes.
8. Mix the contents of the pot with an electric blender.
9. Return the mixture to the same pot on low heat for 5 minutes.
10. Pour it in soup bowls and decorate with lemon slices.

LEVEL OF DIFFICULTY

Oat Soup with Dried Shrimp

SOUPS & SALADS

> My mother used to make Lentil soup for us in the winter, as it brings us warmth and has a distinctive taste.

INGREDIENTS

- 1 cup of instant oat, soaked in 2 cups of warm water
- ½ cup of small dried shrimps (available in Asian shops), cleaned and soaked in water for 15 minutes
- 1 medium onion, finely chopped
- 3 cloves of garlic, crushed
- 5 tablespoons of olive oil
- ½ tablespoon of powdered cumin
- 1 cup of boiling water
- Juice of 1 lemon
- 2 tablespoons of dill, finely chopped
- ¾ tablespoon of salt (or as desired)
- ½ teaspoon of black or red pepper
- Scallion (green onion) for decoration

30+30 minutes PREP TIME + COOKING

DIRECTIONS

1. Put a pot on low heat.
2. Add oil to the pot and fry the onion and the garlic together until they turn golden-colored.
3. Drain the shrimp from its soaking water, add it to the pot and stir for 2 minutes.
4. Add the cumin and the pepper and stir the mix for a minute.
5. Add the soaked oat to the mix and stir well while gradually adding the boiling water.
6. Stir well for three minutes to prevent the oat from bulking up.
7. Leave the pot on low heat for 15 minutes.
8. Add the lemon, the dill and the salt and leave the pot on low heat for 3 more minutes.
9. Pour the soup in the bowl and decorate it with the scallion.

LEVEL OF DIFFICULTY

Fish Soup

SOUPS & SALADS

> Fish soup is one of the soups my mother used to make for us. She was also skilled in making fish Aseeda. Both are delicious, and many flavors are combined in them: the lime's sting, the pepper's heat, the tamarind's sourness and the fish's rich taste.

INGREDIENTS

- 250g of fish slices (boneless supreme fish)
- 2 onions, shredded
- 4 cloves of garlic, shredded
- Juice of 2 red (ripe) tomatoes
- Juice of 1 lime
- 60g of tamarind, soaked in a cup of warm water and strained from impurities (using a mesh strainer)
- ½ pack of fresh coriander, very finely chopped
- 2 tablespoons of dill, finely chopped
- ½ a large whole red bell pepper, blended in a mixer with ½ cup of water and filtered of impurities
- 1 teaspoon of fish spices
- 1 teaspoon of powdered coriander
- 1 teaspoon of powdered cumin
- 1 teaspoon of powdered turmeric
- ½ teaspoon of red chili pepper
- ¾ tablespoon of salt (as desired)
- 1 ½ tablespoon of flour, mixed with ⅓ cup of water
- 1 cup of hot water
- ¼ cup of olive oil

25+30 minutes
PREP TIME + COOKING

DIRECTIONS

1. Put the oil in a pot on medium heat.
2. After 1 minute, add the onion and the garlic and mix for 2 minutes.
3. Add the fish slices and stir for 3 minutes until the fish crumbles.
4. Add the spices, the coriander, the cumin, the turmeric and the red chili pepper and stir.
5. After 1 minute, add the tomato juice and the tamarind infusion (the liquid resulting from the soaking) and stir for 4 minutes.
6. Add the hot water and stir the mix.
7. Add the flour mixture with fast stirring to prevent it from bulking up.
8. Add the coriander, dill, salt and lime juice.
9. Leave it on low heat for 5 minutes.
10. Decorate it with some dill.

Note

The amount of lime juice is left to your taste, and so is the salt.
Adding a cup of hot water depends on the desired soup density. It may be ½ or ¾ cup as desired.

LEVEL OF DIFFICULTY

Onion and Arugula Salad

SOUPS & SALADS

Vegetarian

10+8 minutes PREP TIME + COOKING

INGREDIENTS

- 3 red or white onions
- 1 Pack of small-sized arugula
- 3 large red tomatoes
- Juice of 2 limes
- ½ teaspoon of salt

DIRECTIONS

1. Chop the onion and the tomatoes to slices.
2. Mix the onions, the tomatoes and the arugula.
3. Mix the lime juice with the salt and then pour it on the salad.

LEVEL OF DIFFICULTY

My Mother's Salad

SOUPS & SALADS — Vegetarian

15+6 minutes
PREP TIME + COOKING

INGREDIENTS

- 6 leaves of lettuce, chopped to medium pieces
- 3 tomatoes, chopped to medium cubes
- 5 scallions, chopped to medium pieces
- 2 carrots, chopped to cubes
- 5 leaves of large-sized arugula, chopped to medium pieces
- 2 cucumbers, chopped to medium cubes
- 3 small radishes, chopped to medium cubes
- ½ pack of coriander, chopped
- Juice of 2 limes
- 5 tablespoons of olive oil
- ¼ teaspoon of salt

DIRECTIONS

1. Mix the lime, the oil and the salt well.
2. Put all the other ingredients in a deep container.
3. Pour the lime, oil and salt mixture in the container, stir, and then serve.

LEVEL OF DIFFICULTY

Yogurt Salad

SOUPS & SALADS

Vegetarian

INGREDIENTS

- 2 cups of yogurt
- 1 small onion, finely chopped
- 1 large red tomato
- 1 clove of garlic, crushed
- ½ cup of small cubes of cucumber
- ¼ cup of small cubes of carrots
- ¼ pack of coriander, finely chopped
- ¼ tablespoon of salt

DIRECTIONS

1. Put the yogurt in a deep container, add the salt to it and mix them well.
2. Add all the other ingredients to yoghurt and salt mixture and mix them well, then serve.

Dessert

Desserts in the past used to be made from simple ingredients and presented on special occasions. Over time, modifications were added to their ingredients and preparation methods, and so their taste changed, and in some cases both the taste and form changed. However, I am presenting them to you like my mother used to prepare them in the 1970s, albeit with subtle amendments that I introduced to ease the recipes. Additionally, I used alternatives to some of the ingredients that I assume are not commonly found in global markets.

When making the desserts in this chapter, you can use vegetable oil instead of cow ghee. I, myself often prepare them with corn oil or unsalted butter, and they maintain their good taste. However, my mother used to prepare food with ghee or butter because cows were available at our house.

Her favorite oil among the vegetable oils was olive oil, followed by corn oil. In addition, of course, to the staple ingredients in her desserts; Saffron, cardamom and rosewater, which distinguish the Arab Gulf kitchen in general.

Khanfurush

DESSERT

Vegetarian

» This is a delicious and famous dessert in the Arab Gulf countries. My mother used to prepare it for us using the old traditional method. Over the years though, it was subjected to some additions as it is now presented in various shapes and sizes, and it is also baked in electrical devices.

INGREDIENTS

- 1 ½ cups of rice flour
- ½ cup of all-purpose flour (plain flour)
- 5 eggs, whisked
- 1 ½ tablespoons of instant yeast
- 1 cup of sugar
- 1 teaspoon of powdered cardamom
- ½ teaspoon of saffron
- ¼ cup of rosewater
- ½ cup of frying oil
- 3 tablespoons of sesame
- ¼ cup of water for kneading

60 minutes for dough to set PREP TIME

35-40 minutes COOKING

DIRECTIONS

1. Mix all the dry ingredients together then add the eggs to the dough, which must be mellow.
2. Leave the dough for an hour to set.
3. Put a non-deep pan on the stove and add the oil.
4. After the oil heats, using a spoon or fingertips dipped in oil, take a tablespoon of the dough, put it in the pan, sprinkle sesame on top of it, leave it for around a minute and then flip it in order for both sides to be fried.
5. Repeat the previous step until the dough is finished.
6. After it is done, it may be presented hot or cold, after sprinkling it with powdered sugar.

Note: You may not need the full ¼ cup of water for kneading. Only some of it may be necessary for the dough to become mellow, which depends on the type of flour used.

LEVEL OF DIFFICULTY

DATE AND CHAMI - DESSERT

Luqaimat (Traditional Method)

DESSERT — **Vegetarian**

>> It is a type of Arab Gulf dessert that is inexpensive and prepared in every house, especially on occasions and holidays, and more specially in the month of Ramadan. Some changes were made to it, by adding some new ingredients, which is different than the old traditional method of the 1970s and before. The method I will be presenting is how my mother used to prepare them, with the exception of adding instant yeast, which was not available back then. But the ordinary yeast takes longer to ferment the dough and so I consider this a shortcut and not a modification to the original recipe.

60 minutes for dough to set — PREP TIME
30-40 minutes COOKING

INGREDIENTS

- 1 cup of all-purpose flour
- 1 egg
- 1 ½ tablespoon of instant yeast
- ½ teaspoon of fine cardamom powder
- ¼ teaspoon of saffron
- A sprinkle of salt
- 2 tablespoons of vegetable oil
- 3 tablespoons of sugar
- 3 cups of cow ghee (Available in Asian shops) or vegetable oil
- ¾ cup of warm water for kneading

DIRECTIONS

1. Add all ingredients in a bowl, except water.
2. Add the warm water gradually while you are kneading (by hand), knead the dough well until you get an elastic dough. Leave it to set for one hour, then knead it once more for 2-3 minutes.
3. Put about 3 cups of ghee in a small pot or a deep pan.
4. After the oil heats, dip your fingertips in some oil, then take about ¼ a tablespoon of the dough with your fingertips and drop it in the oil, move it around in the pot/pan so that all sides get fried.
5. Repeat with the remaining dough, frying a group of balls every time until the dough is used up.
6. Pour date molasses or honey on the Loqaimat, sprinkle it with sesame and serve it.

LEVEL OF DIFFICULTY

Quraisat (Diskettes)

DESSERT — Vegetarian

>> People might have different ways to make Quraisat, but my mother used to make them by mixing very finely-chopped onions in the dough. The onions could barely be seen, but were noticed by taste, which enhanced the taste of sugar and salt in the dough. Additionally, their deliciousness was increased after frying them in ghee or oil as they became crispy and golden-colored.

INGREDIENTS

- 2 cups of all-purpose flour
- 1 tablespoon of instant yeast
- 3 tablespoons of sugar
- 2 tablespoons of vegetable oil
- 1 teaspoon of fennel seeds
- 1 teaspoon of salt
- A small onion, finely chopped (around 2 tablespoons)
- 1 cup of warm water for kneading
- ¾ cup of vegetable oil

90 minutes for dough to set — PREP TIME
35 minutes COOKING

DIRECTIONS

1. Mix all of the ingredients together (except the ¾ cup of vegetable oil), knead them together and put the dough in a warm place for an hour and a half.
2. Put a pan on the stove on medium heat and add the oil. After the oil heats, put about a tablespoon of the dough in the oil. After about a minute, flip the diskette over for the other side to be fried. Repeat until the dough is used up.
3. Pour date molasses on it and serve it.

LEVEL OF DIFFICULTY

Qurs Mafrook

(Rubbed Disk) DESERT

Vegetarian

>> *This type of dessert always takes me back to my beautiful childhood! My father used to make this type of dessert for us, and I used to sit by his side watching him making the dough, shaping it into balls, spreading them and baking them, the baking method was strange though. He used to put the charcoal in the furnace and light them up, and then spread the dough into round disks, putting them directly on the hot coals, leaving them to turn red, flip them on the other side and so on until they were done. After they cooled down, he used to put them on a metal tray, sprinkle ghee and sugar on them, cut them by hand and rub them, hence the name, due to rubbing it by hand in order to absorb the ghee properly and make the sugar stick to it. After that, he used to sprinkle fine cardamom powder on the dish and serve it to us. How delicious it was, particularly in the winter!*

I remember, in one occasion, I asked my father about its name, he told me: "It is Qurs Mafrook." And I said, "No. It is Qurs Mahrook (Burnt disk)." He laughed and agreed to the name I gave it. However, after my mother taught me her method of making it, I was convinced that the name Qurs Mafrook was more appropriate for it.

This is my mother's simplified recipe; I am passing it on to you as I have learned it. I hope you enjoy making and eating it. It is presented hot and cold, and it is excellent in the winter, as it will make you warm.

INGREDIENTS

- 2 cups of Chakki Atta flour
- 1 cup of water
- ½ teaspoon of salt
- 1 teaspoon of cardamon seeds
- 1 tsp Saffron
- ½ cup of sugar
- ¼ cup of ghee

30 minutes kneading & dough PREP TIME
35-40 minutes COOKING

DIRECTIONS

1. Mix the salt with the flour and water and knead them until you have a coherent dough.
2. Divide the dough into 6 parts, shape them into balls and spread them into disks with the thickness of ½ an inch each.
3. Bake the disk in a pan after spreading a bit of ghee on it, leave it until it becomes red and then flip it and leave it until the other side reddens as well.
4. After it cools down, cut it by hand, sprinkle ghee and sugar on it, and rub it with your palm until it crumbles.
5. Finally, add the cardamom and Saffron, mix it well and serve it.

LEVEL OF DIFFICULTY

Aseeda Bobbar

DATE AND CHAMI - DESSERT

(Pumpkin Aseeda) — DESSERT

> Aseeda is considered among the popular desserts in the Arab gulf and some Arab countries. It is prepared in many ways and served on holidays and occasions. Here in Dubai we have the regular aseeda, date fruit aseeda and pumpkin aseeda. I chose the pumpkin aseeda because pumpkin is available worldwide.

35 minutes to grill the pumpkin — PREP TIME

35-40 minutes — COOKING

INGREDIENTS

- 1 ¼ cup of Shudh Chakki Atta flour
- ½ cup of ghee
- 1 cup of sugar (or as desired)
- ¼ cup of rosewater with ½ teaspoon of saffron soaked in it
- 1 tablespoon of fine cardamom powder
- 1 teaspoon of ginger powder
- 1 teaspoon of fennel powder
- 1 average-sized pumpkin (1 kg)
- 2 ½ cup of water to mix the flour

DIRECTIONS

1. Cut the pumpkin in half and grill it in the oven for 35 minutes until it is cooked without burning. After it cools down, remove the crust and seeds, and scoop out the flesh. Its texture would be puree-like.
2. Roast the flour in a pan for 8 minutes until it becomes blonde-colored, leave it to cool down.
3. Sift the flour to get rid of any impurities and put it in a bowl. Pour 2 and ½ cups of water on it and mix it well.
4. Then add the puree pumpkin to the flour-water mix, mix them until they blend together without any bulky masses, and set the mixture aside.
5. Put a dry and clean pot on the stove, put the sugar in it and stir it until it caramelizes. It should be on medium heat so as not to burn.
6. Then add 1 and ½ cups of boiling water to the pot, and let it simmer until the caramelized sugar dissolves completely.
7. Add the cardamom, ginger, fennel and ghee and let them boil for 5 minutes. Then add the mixture of flour, pumpkin and water gradually with continuous stirring. Finally, add the rosewater and saffron, and keep stirring until the aseeda has a somewhat dense texture. Leave it on very low heat for 7 minutes so as not to burn.
8. Pour it in a serving plate and decorate with any type of nuts you prefer.

Note: The overall cooking time may take an hour or bit longer depending on the hardness of the pumpkin, therefore, a pressure cooker could be used to save time and effort.

LEVEL OF DIFFICULTY: ★★ (2 of 3)

Sago

DESSERT — **Vegetarian**

>> *My mother used to make sago for us early in the morning and serve it to us for breakfast. She used to prepare it in two ways: with milk in summer, and the regular one in Ramadan and in winter. The regular one is quite common in the Arab Gulf countries. I noticed that sago is also known and eaten in Asian countries, though with different methods, and it has many names.*

INGREDIENTS

- 1 cup of sago pearls (washed and soaked in 2 cups of water for 15 minutes)
- 1 teaspoon of cardamom powder soaked in ¼ cup of rosewater
- 1 teaspoon of saffron soaked in ¼ cup of rosewater
- ¼ cup of ghee or corn oil
- 1 cup of sugar (or as desired)
- 2 ½ cups of boiling water

DIRECTIONS

1. Put a pot on low heat, put the sugar in it and stir it until it caramelizes.
2. Add the water to it (after the sugar reaches the boiling point) and stir until the sugar dissolves completely.
3. Add the cardamom and the ghee to the pot and stir for 2-3 minutes.
4. Add the soaked sago with its water (the water it was soaked in) to the pot and stir continuously in order for the mix not to bulk up and in order for the white sago pearls to become gelatinous and coherent.
5. Add the rosewater and saffron, and stir to blend it with the sago, leave the mixture on low heat for 5 minutes so as not to burn it.
6. When serving, decorate it with saffron strings, fine cardamom powder or ghee.

DATE AND CHAMI - DESSERT

Sago with Milk

DESSERT — **Vegetarian**

>> *This method is not that different from the previous one. My mother used to make it for us with fresh cow milk, and we used to eat it warm or cold. She also used to put it in cups and keep it in the fridge. This was in the early 1970s, after we had gotten a fridge in our house.*

INGREDIENTS

- ¾ cup of sago pearls (soaked in water for 15 minutes)
- ¾ cup of sugar (or as desired)
- 5 cups of liquid milk
- ½ teaspoon of saffron (soaked in ¼ cup of rosewater)

15 minutes for soaking pearls — PREP TIME
30 minutes COOKING

DIRECTIONS

1. Put the pot on a stove on low heat and pour the milk in it. After it boils, add to it the soaked sago (after straining it of water) and stir.
2. After 10 minutes, add the sugar and cardamom and keep stirring.
3. After the sago pearls become gelatinous, add the saffron and rosewater. Keep stirring for three minutes until the components blend and become coherent.
4. Leave it on very low heat for 8 minutes.
5. Pour it in glasses and decorate the top. My mother used to decorate it with almonds or pistachios.

LEVEL OF DIFFICULTY

DATE AND CHAMI - DESSERT

Khabees

DESSERT

> In my childhood, when I caught the smell of roasting the flour filling our house, I used to run to the kitchen to ask my mother: "Are you going to make us Aseeda or Khabees?" She used to answer me with a smile and say: "Which do you prefer?" I used to leave it up to her because I know well that my mother is skilled in making both of them!

INGREDIENTS

- 2 cups of Chakki Atta flour
- 2 cups of water
- 1 cup of sugar
- ½ cup of ghee or vegetable oil
- ¼ cup of rosewater
- 1 tablespoon of cardamom powder
- 1 teaspoon of saffron

DIRECTIONS

1. Put the saffron in the rosewater and keep it aside until the mixture becomes yellow-colored.
2. Put the flour in a non-stick pot on low-heat and stir the flour for 10 minutes until it becomes brown-colored.
3. Sift the flour after roasting it to get rid of impurities.
4. In another pot, put the water and sugar on the stove until the sugar dissolves completely.
5. Return the flour to the pot it was roasted in, add the ghee on it, mix them together until they blend well, and sprinkle the cardamom on them.
6. Put the pot on low heat, and gradually add the boiling water -sugar mixture to the flour with stirring until all the water is added.
7. Sprinkle the saffron-rose water mix on the mixture and stir, leave it on low heat for 5 to 10 minutes.
8. Serve it as or decorated with nuts, we usually have it with Arabian coffee.

Note

The flour should be roasted on low heat, in order for it to be roasted without burning.
When pouring the sugar and water mixture, it should be done gradually, and not all at once.
If some masses form, do not be alarmed and keep stirring, and the flour will eventually mix with the water and sugar. At this stage, the Khabees will begin emitting its sweet smell.

Bathitha

DESSERT

> Bathitha is a traditional dessert that consists mainly of flour and dates. My father told me that the Bathitha used to be their companion in the journeys of diving in search of pearls, which could extend to four months (from May to September), and it remained valid until the end of the diving journey. Now, it has become the companion of travelers, and it is also served to guests or shared with family and friends.

INGREDIENTS

- 2 cups of all-purpose flour
- 2 cups of pitted dates
- 1 tablespoon of cardamom powder
- 1 tablespoon of fennel powder
- 1 tablespoon of ginger powder
- ¾ cup of cow ghee
- Flaked almond or pistachio

DIRECTIONS

1. Fry the flour in a pan on the stove until it becomes blonde-colored.
2. Put the seedless dates in a pot and sift the flour over it to get rid of any impurities.
3. Pour the ghee on the dates and flour, and begin mixing the dates, flour and ghee by hand until they mix well.
4. Add the cardamom, fennel and ginger and mix them well by hand.
5. Put the Bathitha in a container, decorate it with almonds or pistachios and close the container tightly, if kept in an airtight container, it stays valid for months. We usually have it with Arabian coffee.

DATE AND CHAMI - DESSERT

Farni

DESSERT — Vegetarian

>> This type of dessert is usually made in the month of Ramadan, i.e. at sunset, after the fasting hours pass. I remember from my childhood that before the month of Ramadan, my mother used to wash a large amount of rice, about 4 kilograms, and take it to the miller to be milled, so that she can use it to prepare Farny in Ramadan. Families exchange desserts in the month of Ramadan, and Muhallebi is one of the most exchanged desserts.

INGREDIENTS

- 1 liter of fresh milk
- ½ cup of milled (ground) rice
- ¼ cup of sugar
- ¼ teaspoon of saffron
- ¼ cup of rosewater with half the amount of saffron soaked in it

10+30 minutes PREP TIME + COOKING

DIRECTIONS

1. Pour the milk in a pot on medium heat, add to it the milled rice and the sugar.
2. Stir continuously to avoid bulking up, until the mixture thickens.
3. Add the rosewater and the saffron, and after stirring for few minutes, leave it on low heat for two more minutes without covering.
4. Pour it in deep bowls or cups and decorate it with saffron strings.

Note: I find this a very likeable dish for children
The ¼ teaspoon of saffron is divided between the rosewater and decoration.

LEVEL OF DIFFICULTY

Rushufa

DESSERT — Vegetarian

>> Here, I will break my habit with you. The one who used to prepare this dish is my father, and not my mother. Despite her skill in making it, she used to leave it up to him as he enjoyed preparing it. Its name is derived from the word (Rashaf: to sip)

INGREDIENTS

20+30 minutes PREP TIME + COOKING

- ½ cup of Chakki Atta flour, roasted until it becomes blonde-colored
- 1 tablespoon of cardamom powder
- 1 tablespoon of ginger powder
- ¼ tablespoon of cinnamon powder
- ¼ teaspoon of black pepper
- ½ teaspoon of turmeric
- ½ cup of sugar (or as desired)
- 5 cups of hot water
- 5 tablespoons of butter or corn oil
- 3 tablespoons of flaked almonds

DIRECTIONS

1. Sift the flour to remove impurities.
2. Put a pot on low heat, put the roasted flour and the butter/oil in it, and stir until they all blend together.
3. Add the cardamom, ginger, cinnamon, black pepper and turmeric, and stir well until they all blend together.
4. Begin pouring the hot water while stirring continuously with a hand blender to avoid bulking up.
5. Add the sugar and let the mixture simmer for 20 minutes.
6. Crumble the almond flakes by hand and add them to the mix.
7. Pour it in cups and serve it.

Note: Rashufa is similar to soup in structure and it is very suitable for cold dark winters.

LEVEL OF DIFFICULTY

DATE AND CHAMI - DESSERT

Beverages

Arabic Coffee

BEVERAGES

 Vegetarian

> We have two main variants of Arabic coffee in the Arab gulf countries, one is yellow in color and light in taste while the other has a dark brown color and its flavor tends to be concentrated and bitter. The coffee's color and bitterness depend on its method of roasting and the added spices. I personally prefer it yellow and light.
>
> In general, Arabic coffee is prepared with cardamom and saffron, which add to it a special flavor and a sweet fragrance. Sometimes rosewater is also added to it, especially on holidays and special occasions. Some people flavor it only with cardamom, while there are others who prepare it with clove only; each according to their own taste.

INGREDIENTS

- 3 cups of water
- 2 tablespoons of coffee, roasted and grounded
- 1 tablespoon of powdered cardamom
- ¾ teaspoon of saffron

5+10 minutes
PREP TIME + COOKING

DIRECTIONS

1. Pour the water in a kettle and put it on medium heat for 4 minutes.
2. Add the coffee and turn the heat down to low. Keep for 6 more minutes.
3. Turn the stove off and leave the kettle aside for a while until the coffee settles in the bottom of the kettle.
4. Put the cardamom and the saffron in the thermos.
5. Pour the coffee (over the cardamom and saffron) in the thermos coffee pot.
6. Serve with date fruits and various sweets.

LEVEL OF DIFFICULTY

Milk Tea

BEVERAGES

> Milk tea has existed in our cuisine for decades, however, in the present time, the method of its preparation has changed, and it is now locally called Karak. Originally, the Karak recipe came to us from the Indian kitchen, due to our interaction with the Indian people. In Karak, the fresh milk is replaced with evaporated milk, and in addition to cardamom and saffron, ginger, clove and cinnamon are sometimes added to it. Karak is now heavily consumed in my country and so many people start their days with a cup of the creamy and flavorful Karak. The recipe for milk tea that I am presenting here though is the one that my mother used to follow before the prevalence of Karak in the country.

INGREDIENTS

- 4 cups of fresh milk
- 1 ½ tablespoons of black tea
- 1 teaspoon of rough powdered cardamom
- 4 tablespoons of sugar (or as desired)
- ½ teaspoon of saffron

DIRECTIONS

1. Put the fresh milk and the tea in the pot on medium heat.
2. Shortly after it boils, add the cardamom, saffron and sugar.
3. Stir for a while, turn the heat down to low and leave it for 5 minutes.
4. Put a small sieve on the thermos opening and pour the milk tea through it in the thermos.

Milk with Saffron and Cardamom

BEVERAGES  **Vegetarian**

>> *Since we had cows in our house, my mother used to use their milk in preparing all kinds of flavored milk and desserts. One such recipe is milk with saffron and cardamom.*

INGREDIENTS

- 4 cups of fresh milk
- 1 teaspoon of rough powdered cardamom
- ½ teaspoon of saffron
- 4 tablespoons of sugar (or as desired)

DIRECTIONS

1. Put the milk and the cardamon in a pot on medium heat.
2. When it boils, add the sugar and stir for a while.
3. Leave it for 3 minutes on low heat.
4. Put the saffron in the thermos.
5. Put a small sieve on the thermos opening and pour the milk through it in the thermos.
6. Serve in the morning, in the evening and also for guests.

LEVEL OF DIFFICULTY

Ginger Milk

BEVERAGES

Vegetarian

>> *My mother used to make this type of milk for us in winter time, in order to give us warmth in addition to enjoying its distinctive flavor and spicy taste.*

- 4 cups of fresh milk
- 4 tablespoons of sugar (or as desired)
- 20g of dry ginger - ground with the mortar and pestle

1. Put the pot with the milk in it on medium heat.
2. When it boils, add the ginger and the sugar and turn the heat down to low.
3. After 5 minutes, the milk and the ginger will have intermixed.
4. Turn off the stove and leave it set for 2 minutes.
5. Put the sieve on the thermos opening, and pour the milk through the sieve in the thermos.

 *The ginger is ground in the mortar and not powdered (merely to crumble its tissues). This will make its taste better than using powdered ginger.*

Lumi (Lime) Tea

BEVERAGES

 Vegetarian

>> In this type of tea, the lime's sourness and nice smell mixes with the sugar, making its drinker feel refreshed and filled with positive energy. This beverage is from my country's heritage.

INGREDIENTS

- 3 cups of water
- 2 dry limes, washed, incised with knife and its seeds removed
- 5 tablespoons of sugar
- 1 tablespoon of rosewater

DIRECTIONS

1. Put the pot containing the water on medium heat.
2. Before it begins boiling, put the lime.
3. Let it boil for 4 minutes on low heat.
4. Add the sugar and stir for a while.
5. After 2 minutes, turn off the stove.
6. Add the rosewater.
7. Pour it in serving cups.

Note: The amount of sugar is as desired (it is tastier with little sugar) In the Arab Gulf, we call the lime, especially dried lime (Lumi).

8+15 minutes PREP TIME + COOKING

LEVEL OF DIFFICULTY

DATE AND CHAMI - BEVERAGES 137

Cardamom and Saffron Tea

BEVERAGES • Vegetarian

>> My children and I prefer this kind of tea over regular tea, because it reminds us of the days when my mother used to make it for us. It has a refined and exclusive taste.

INGREDIENTS

- 4 cups of water
- 2 tablespoons of black tea
- 3 ½ tablespoons of sugar (or as desired)
- 1 teaspoon of rough powdered cardamom
- ½ teaspoon of saffron

5+10 minutes PREP TIME + COOKING

DIRECTIONS

1. Put a pot containing the water on medium heat until it boils.
2. Add the tea and the cardamom, and turn the heat down to low.
3. Two minutes later, add the sugar and stir for a while (leave it for 2 minutes).
4. Put the saffron in the thermos.
5. Put the sieve on the thermos opening and pour the tea through it in the thermos.

Note: We drink cardamom and saffron tea with nuts or biscuits, and we serve it to guests on various occasions.

LEVEL OF DIFFICULTY

Milk with Thyme

BEVERAGES

Vegetarian

>> My mother used to make us this drink with milk to warm us up in the winter, and without milk as a remedy for cold and cough.

INGREDIENTS

- 3 cups of fresh milk
- 2 tablespoons of sugar (or as desired)
- 1 tablespoon of thyme (Thymus serpyllum)

5+10 minutes
PREP TIME + COOKING

DIRECTIONS

1. Put the milk in a pot on medium heat until it begins to boil.
2. Add the thyme and leave it for 5 minutes on low heat.
3. Add the sugar and stir for a while, then leave it for 2 minutes.
4. Pour it in serving cups through a sieve.

Note: Thyme must be washed beforehand.

LEVEL OF DIFFICULTY: ★

DATE AND CHAMI - BEVERAGES

Laban (Yogurt Drink)

BEVERAGES  Vegetarian

> My mother used to make yogurt from cow milk. After milking the cow, she used to remove the foam from the milk, put it in a container (Mallah), cover it with a piece of cloth made from light cotton and put it on a shelf made from four pillars, which she hung to a branch of the almond tree, which is called (Midah). In the early morning, she put the resulting yogurt in a container (Saqqa), which used to be made from sheep skin, but it was then developed to be made from metal, which is the version I witnessed. The Saqqa is hung in three pieces of wood forming a triangle and called (Shayb). My mother sat to shake it until cream formed, and this required a lot of her time and effort. The result of shaking is a dense milk (Laban) and a layer of cream. After that, my mother used to seperate the cream from the Laban, put the Laban in a pot made from metal, add salt to it and present it to us as a delicious and healthy beverage. She also used to make Chami from the remainder of it.

Laban is considered the favorite beverage for all Arab Gulf nationals, particularly with lunch or dinner that consists of meat or chicken. Dried mint, powdered fenugreek, red pepper or cumin may be added to it as desired.

INGREDIENTS

- 1kg of yogurt
- ¾ tablespoon of salt (or as desired)
- 4 cups of water

5+10 minutes
PREP TIME + COOKING

DIRECTIONS

1. Mix the yogurt and water well with a hand blender to obtain Laban.
2. Add the salt and mix it in well.
3. Pour it in a glass jug or bottle.
4. Put it in the fridge until serving it or making Chami from it.

LEVEL OF DIFFICULTY

Red lentil

Sago

Balaleet vermicilli

Dried lumi (lime)

Dango

Split chickpeas

Dried round chilli

Pantry staples

Homemade Ghee

PANTRY STAPLES **Vegetarian**

>> No house in the Arab Gulf can be found without our flavored ghee, it is a staple ingredient in our cuisine that used to be solely made at homes but is now readily available in supermarkets and groceries. As it is flavored with different spices, it has a distinctive taste that adds unparallel richness and deliciousness to many dishes.

At our home when I was little, my mother used to collect the butter that forms when shaking the milk (i.e. when making Laban), put it in a clear container, and sprinkle it with salt to prevent it from going bad. After a week of collecting the butter, she used to turn it into ghee, filter it and pour it in a container called Keraz, which was used specifically for this purpose.

INGREDIENTS

- 2-500g packets of salted butter
- 2 tablespoons of flour
- 2 tablespoons of coriander seeds, roughly grounded
- 2 tablespoons of cumin seeds, roughly grounded
- 2 tablespoons of fennel seeds, roughly grounded
- ¼ teaspoon of turmeric powder

DIRECTIONS

1. Roast the flour in a pot on low heat until it turns to a light brown color.
2. Add the spices and mix them with the flour for 1 minute.
3. Add the butter to the pot and once it melts, mix it well with the flour.
4. Let the mixture boil until the foam disappears completely (depending on the type of butter, this step could take up to 30-45 minutes).
5. After it cools down completely and before it solidifies pour it through a sieve in a clean and dry glass jar until it is time to use it.

LEVEL OF DIFFICULTY

Note: The pot used for making ghee must be clean from the smells of other food. This ghee can be stored in room temperature as there is no need to refrigerate it.

Bzaar

PANTRY STAPLES

Vegetarian

>> Bzaar is the spice mix used in the majority of our savory dishes. It is like the five-spice for the Chinese or the Garam masala for the Indians. The recipe for Bzaar varies from one house to another depending on the taste preferences of that household. In general though, the ingredients for Bezaar are similar. This recipe for Bazaar is my mother's, for she used to make it herself to make sure it is as she likes it, in order to give our dishes her own flavor.

INGREDIENTS

- 2 tablespoons of coriander seeds.
- 1 ½ tablespoons of cumin
- 1 cinnamon whole
- 1 teaspoon of black pepper
- 1 tablespoon of dried garlic slices
- 1 tablespoon of (organic) powdered turmeric
- 1 ½ tablespoons of cardamom

DIRECTIONS

1. Break the cinnamon to 5cm pieces.
2. Put a pan on low heat, and add the cinnamon, the cardamom and the black pepper in the pan with stirring.
3. After 3 minutes, put the remaining ingredients, except the turmeric, with stirring.
4. After 2-3 minutes, the fragrance will start spreading in the air, so turn off the stove.
5. Let it cool down completely.
6. Grind it in an electronic coffee and spice grinder.
7. Put the resulting powder in a container, add the turmeric to it and mix them well.
8. Put it in a glass container and close it tightly.

Daqqus

PANTRY STAPLES

Vegetarian

INGREDIENTS

- 5 tomatoes chopped and pureed in an electric blender
- 3 cloves of garlic mashed
- 2 red hot peppers, finely chopped
- 2 tablespoons finely chopped coriander
- ½ teaspoon cumin powder
- 4 tablespoons olive oil
- 2 tablespoons tomato paste
- ½ teaspoon salt or as desired

10+15 minutes
PREP TIME + COOKING

DIRECTIONS

1. Put a pot on medium heat, add the olive oil to it.
2. Add the garlic to the pot and stir until it turns golden-colored (around 3 minutes).
3. Add the remaining ingredients except the salt and stir well.
4. Add the salt and keep the mixture on low heat for around 4 minutes.

LEVEL OF DIFFICULTY

Story

Ever since my childhood, I have been always fond of the act of cooking and immersing myself in the culinary world. As a child, I used to spend good portions of my days watching my mother being involved in food related activities; milking her cows, collecting eggs from under our hens, making butter and Laban, grinding and mixing her own spices, roasting coffee and of course cooking our meals. Watching her filled me with joy and I used to try to imitate her whenever a chance came up.

One memory that I remember vividly happened on a weekend afternoon when I was around seven. While I was playing with my friends in the courtyard in front of our house, I spotted my mother leaving the house to visit one of her friends. I immediately seized the opportunity, left my friends and hurried towards our kitchen so excited that I would finally be able to cook something and surprise my mother. However, the surprise was mine as I found myself in a kitchen with no knives and matchboxes. It turned out that me mother had hid them fearing that I might hurt myself for she expected that I would run into the kitchen as soon as she was out of the door. When I turned ten my mother finally gave me the permission to start cooking our traditional dishes and to experiment in the kitchen myself, and that was where my love for cooking started flourishing and evolving.

The traditional dishes that I used to prepare with my mother were delicious and unique. Unfortunately, in recent years, some of our traditional dishes underwent radical changes under the pretext of development. I do not mind some renewal, development or facilitation, but not to the point of making these dishes lose their traditional identity. This was my main motivation to write this book that presents our traditional dishes in their authentic flavor in order to preserve our inherited recipes. As for me, the recipes in the book also have a sentimental value as they are mostly based on recipes passed down to me from my mother and that I would like to pass to the next generations and spread around the world.

www.ingramcontent.com/pod-product-compliance
Lightning Source LLC
Chambersburg PA
CBHW041520220426
43667CB00003B/55